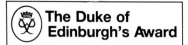

The Duke of
Edinburgh's Award

WORKSHOP

DESIGN & MAKE EXPEDITION EQUIPMENT

DON ROBERTSON

Edited by Nicholas Gair

The Duke of Edinburgh's Award
5 Prince of Wales Terrace
Kensington, London W8 5PG

First edition May 1989

Typeset, printed and bound in Great Britain by
Jolly & Barber Ltd, Rugby, Warwickshire

Designed by Richard Brown FCSD

ISBN 0 905425 07 3 (Hardback)
ISBN 0 905425 08 1 (Softback)

British Railways Board

Sir Robert Reid, CBE, FCIT
Chairman

When the early explorers first set out,
commercially produced clothing did not exist.
Specialist items had to be adapted and improvised
or they simply made their own. Whilst not
neglecting their safety, young people are, through
this book, encouraged to follow this practice by
designing and making their own expedition
equipment.

This has many benefits. It enables young people
to appreciate the function of their clothing,
makes them more discerning customers when
purchasing equipment and makes the planning for
their expeditions into a more extended and
enjoyable project.

Expeditioning should provide a whole experience
rather than just short term instant adventure.
Often the planning and preparing for a journey can
almost be the most exciting and stimulating part
of the exercise. Through learning to design, test
and improve their equipment I am sure that this
book will add considerably to the sense of
achievement which young people can experience by
journeying in the country.

I am delighted, therefore, that British Rail,
through the Community Unit, is able to assist in
this process by sponsoring this publication.

BOB REID

ACKNOWLEDGEMENTS

So many people have added to the fountain of knowledge that is now distilled into this book that it would be impossible to name them all.

I must, however, thank John McLeod who typed the first words on the Word Processor and has been a tower of strength at all times.

Thanks to my daughter Fiona who has typed most of the book.

Finally, my sincere thanks to Eileen M. Clarke for the marvellous art work; Richard Brown for the design; Mike Blisset, Bob Pettigrew, Burberry Ltd, Chris Davies, Kent County Council, Department of Education and Science, John Anderson and the pupils of Kent College, Canterbury for the photographs, which are gratefully acknowledged, without all of whose efforts the book would just be a jumble of words.

Above all, I am deeply grateful for the very special contribution made by the generosity of the British Rail Community Unit, and the support and interest of Sir Robert Reid, Trevor Toolan Managing Director, Personnel and James Crowe the Unit Manager, which has made this book possible.

DEDICATION

I would like to dedicate this Book to my Parents Mr W.M. (Jock) Robertson and Mrs Annie (Lloyd) Robertson who instilled in me, at a very early age, the desire to make things. Also to the beautiful village of Poynton in Cheshire where I learned to love the Great Outdoors.

Contents

Foreword

Every expedition involves careful long term planning, whether it
be an overnight journey in the open countryside of the UK or a
major venture to the wild and hostile regions of the world lasting
several months. The gradual selection and collection of clothing
and equipment is a vital part of this process and one which cannot
be accomplished overnight or, worse, during the afternoon before
boarding the mini-bus for your destination.

Designing, making and testing your own equipment can be a
major part of the long term preparation for any venture and the
sense of achievement when you ultimately fulfil the purpose of
your expedition will be heightened by knowing that you have
made the clothing, which has made it all possible, yourself.

This process also develops an interest in the commercial
manufacture and design of equipment which leads to a better
understanding of its use and, therefore, helps you to ensure that it
will do its job and not let you down at the vital moment. This is
especially important when you are likely to encounter extremes
of temperature and climate, as I have in my expeditions to the
Arctic and Antarctic, where a failure with your equipment could,
quite literally, be a matter of life or death.

Whilst I am not suggesting that everyone immediately sets off to
walk to the Poles in their newly made gaiters and waterproofs, I
do strongly believe that the qualifying venture for your Award

should be a starting point, not an ending, and that you can use the experiences and training you have gained to plan exciting journeys of your own throughout your life. I hope that this book will stimulate you to attempt the manufacture of expedition equipment, both the items described and illustrated and items of your own design. Remember, the planning and preparation for a venture can be as challenging as the journey!

Robert Swan, Polar Explorer

Introduction

It would be quite reasonable to ask why anyone should want to make equipment, especially clothing, for use in the great outdoors. Looking through the numerous monthly magazines on camping, walking, caravanning and the like, one can read pages of advertisements selling every conceivable item for use in the outdoors. In one of the magazines recently, 200 different sleeping bags were examined and reviewed. In another camping magazine, 600 different tents are listed. You only have to walk through any of the large stores to see the vast range of clothing that has been developed for ski-ing and similar winter activities.

Most authors make excuses for writing books but I believe that the prime reason for most authors is that each book is a sort of ego trip for them. I hope, however, that by the time you have read this particular book you will be convinced that there is some logic in providing a book on this topic for a Scheme like The Duke of Edinburgh's Award, and I also hope that people not involved in the Award Scheme will have benefited from the facts contained within the book.

Living in Hampshire in the early 1960's, I had the good fortune to meet a person called Bob Pettigrew, who, at that time, was the Adviser for Outdoor Education in Hampshire. Bob, in spite of having several years experience and being an authority on the Himalayas, still managed to find time and the enthusiasm to encourage school children to take part in The Duke of Edinburgh's Award expeditions to places like the New Forest or, further afield, to the mountains of Wales. I used to go and visit schools in Hampshire with Bob when we were trying to encourage people to take part in the Award Scheme, especially the expedition side. We became very frustrated to find many of them who were quite keen to take children into the outdoors would say to us "but we haven't any gear". Or perhaps we would be running training expeditions for a Bronze or Silver Award at a fixed camp site in the New Forest and it was quite pathetic to see the equipment that children produced to wear during such a journey. I still have examples of the type of thing that they would produce to wear on an expedition which was quite a simple thing in the New Forest. Some of them were plastic mackintoshes which were quite adequate when new, but were rapidly torn to shreds by the activity of the children in the Forest. At best, someone would have dad's old army anorak which, in its day, was very waterproof and adequate but, by the time Johnny was wearing it, would let rain through rather like a sieve.

So between us, Bob and I devised a project called "Expedition Workshop" which was a series of courses run mainly for teachers or youth leaders where we would show them how to make basic equipment for expeditions. The initial object was to show that it was possible to make a good waterproof anorak and trousers. You may think that this was a pretty simple and obvious project to try in the education system, but I can assure you that it took many hours of hard work and talking to convince people that a workshop of this type could be run in schools. Even today, nearly 30 years later, very few people have even thought about trying to make a waterproof jacket and trousers, mainly because the basic materials have never been easily available. Attitude of mind also comes into the picture because you find many people have made a wet suit for themselves which is far more difficult to make than a simple anorak.

The first reason for making equipment is financial and I hope that, by the end of this book, you will appreciate that it is possible to make high-quality clothing and equipment for use in the outdoors at a fraction of the cost that you would pay in a retail shop. That was the original object of the Expedition Workshops in Hampshire and it is still valid today.

The second reason for producing the book is that it is possible under The Duke of Edinburgh's Award to make items of equipment that will be assessed as part of the Skills Section of the Scheme.

With the best will in the world, it is not possible to enjoy the pleasures of outdoor activities all the year round unless one is a member of the SAS or a similar hardened individual. The planning, design and makeup of equipment during the winter is a very satisfactory reason to keep an outdoor club open during the winter months and with the carrot dangling ahead of the members that the finished garments and equipment will be worn on the hills, or in boats, when the weather improves.

Taking education in its widest aspect, there is no doubt at all that anyone who has been involved in designing and making equipment will, in the end, be a much more discerning purchaser of such equipment. I have found that it is surprising how much more critical people become looking at stitching, finishing, quality of zips and the like, when they have been involved in making such items.

This book is not a text book about sewing, but much more a book about self awareness, self expression or creativity, that is in keeping with the best ideals expressed in The Duke of Edinburgh's Award. No one is born knowing how to sew. Humans have a large brain which has very few inborn ideas but is capable of very quickly learning new and complex skills. Learning to sew is on a par with learning to drive a car which psychologists tell us is within the physical and mental capabilities of 90% of the adults in Britain. The difference is that people really want, and very often have to learn, to drive a car.

I have found the designing, making and using many items of equipment, which I make much more as a bodger than as a craftsman, very satisfying in a creative sense. I hope that after reading the book you will go on and have the desire to join in this process of creating and designing items of equipment and that you will find a measure of the satisfaction and pleasure that I have had being involved with Expedition Workshop over the past 30 years. I do not believe for one moment anyone who says that "I cannot sew". What I feel they are really saying is "I don't want to sew".

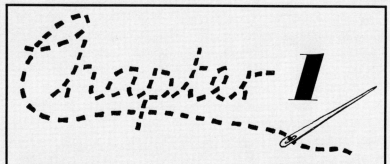

WHAT EQUIPMENT
TO MAKE

The Duke of Edinburgh's Award is keen that you should try to make items of clothing and equipment to use out of doors and in fact you can use the making of some of these items as part of your expedition project. From the contents of the book you will be made aware that I am also very keen on the design and making of all types of equipment. In fact over the years I have made nearly every item of clothing and equipment that you can think of for use in camping, hill walking or sailing.

We must start with a statement about safety and say that there are just a few items of equipment that we would not recommend that you make for yourself. If you make an anorak and the seams leak, you go home and you are wet. If you make a tent and the stitching is not very good, you wake up and have a wet sleeping bag and not much sleep that night. But if you make a carabiner or a piton for rock climbing or a life-jacket for use at sea and these items fail, then you go home in a wooden box. Your mum, dad, teacher, headmaster or youth leader are going to be embarrassed that your item of home-made equipment has resulted in a fatal accident. So we must stress that a few items, if they fail, could result in a serious, or even a fatal, accident and we do not, therefore, recommend that you try and make these at home.

There are very few items of clothing and equipment that cannot, however, be made at home to a very high standard and I have managed to make nearly every type of equipment to use outdoors on the hills or at sea except, I think, boots. Although you do save money by making your own equipment, I have found that the creative satisfaction of making all sorts of items has given me the greatest pleasure. I am afraid it has become something of a family joke that when we are out shopping, my children will come up and see me staring into the window of some large store exhibiting equipment for the outdoors and say "Don't tell us dad, you could make it better"! I am afraid my children consider that this making and designing of equipment is an ego trip for dad to show the world that he can do it better than they can and, if one is analytical about oneself, I suppose there is some element of truth in that statement.

I have always been interested in history and we all have to admit that whatever field of expertise we work in we are standing on the shoulders of countless generations before us. I would like therefore to pay tribute to the man I consider to be the father of modern design, making and testing of all kinds of equipment. Mr Deryck Siddal was Senior Teacher in Physical Education at the King's School in Macclesfield. He came back after serving through World War II and, having had many terrible experiences, merely wanted to settle back to teaching children how to enjoy the pleasures of the great outdoors. He proceeded to establish projects carried out by the children of King's School in developing and testing an enormous range of different items of equipment. He examined the effects of using hot drying rooms to dry out tents, he investigated the sale of sleeping bags and found that the market was in a pretty poor state, with the purchaser not knowing the nature of the filling in the sleeping bag, he then proceeded to design and test a new form of sleeping bag which, in fact, was taken up by one of the manufacturers. He looked at boots, designed new canoe paddle blades and he investigated the effectiveness of boiling water before drinking. The reason you have never heard about Mr Siddal is that coming back from the War, he took a positive decision not to encourage publicity as he merely wanted to get on with teaching the boys at King's School, Macclesfield.

The reason I started making equipment is a complex problem but initially it must have been lack of money. I was lucky enough to spend my childhood in a beautiful village called Poynton in Cheshire, which nestles in the foothills of the Peak District and, there, the hills beckoned me constantly as a boy. I knew, however, that there was no possibility of buying equipment so I suppose we just had to make things. Luckily 90% of boys in those days went to school with hobnail boots and everybody would have a mackintosh because nobody had a car and we had to brave the weather of the north of England. Also in Poynton in those days, sewing was a way of life because the firm of E & R Buck Ltd founded their first factory there. The trade mark 'Bukta' was widely known in swimwear, football equipment and tents.

Eventually graduating in Human Physiology but determined to make a career in research, financial necessity, that is the need to pay the mortgage, forced me to take a job quickly and the only one that looked interesting was in a small village near Poynton called Bollington, where the Rock Bank Research Establishment

had been set up by a company at the turn of the century. Rock
Bank Research Establishment was a big old house and had, since
1900, been responsible for producing many of the standard tests
concerned with spinning and weaving cotton. When I joined the
Establishment there was a second industrial revolution taking
place with the introduction of man-made fibres. Although nylon
had been made since 1938, the Second World War had absorbed
most of the production, and it was only in the late 1950s that the
fibres we all take for granted today were being expanded into
civilian garments. Thinking that the salary would pay the
mortgage for a month or two, I found the work so interesting that,
in fact, I stayed five years and had, in that time, a good grounding
in the technology associated with all forms of textiles. We did not
handle anything to do with wool as this was always dealt with on
the other side of the Pennines in Yorkshire. The combination of
five years experience in textiles research and the Degree in Human
Physiology eventually was responsible for my moving to
Farnborough to work in research connected with human
physiology, especially the effects of heat and cold on men.
Inevitably, I was drawn into the design of clothing to combat
heat and cold stress and so have evolved a wide experience in
dealing with modern materials.

So the author is a human physiologist with many years experience
in designing specialist clothing for all types of jobs and purposes
but is only an amateur at sewing. I believe that having no formal
training in the art of sewing makes one more creative because one
is less inhibited.

Looking at the magazines, that were few and far between anyway,
that had an interest in outdoor sports, for example the *Geographical
Magazine* or *Journal of the Alpine Club* in London, for the years
between the First World War and the Second World War, you
would find very little equipment offered for sale. Speaking to
people who went expeditioning in this era, they often had to, for
example, go to a saddler and ask him to make them a rucksac.
Odd firms were offering a limited range of tents which looked
very much like the ones used today by Scouts and Guides. One of
the few shops that you would have found that kept any sort of
specialist equipment was owned by Mr Robert Lawrie who, from
54 Seymour Street, London W1, which is a little street off Oxford

Street in London, has supplied expeditions for over 50 years with high quality specialist equipment. 54 Seymour Street was in fact where Mr Lawrie lived and the shop consisted of the two ground floor rooms of his house and home.

Looking at photographs of the members of the early Everest Expeditions, it is pretty obvious that there was no specialised equipment because they all look pretty scruffy and seem to be wearing a variety of garments. For example, we have Colonel Norton leading the Everest Expedition in 1924 and still managing to get to 28,000 feet wearing a heavy duty Norfolk jacket and trousers, admittedly lined with flannel with a floppy felt hat, and wearing hobnail boots. He reached 28,000 feet without oxygen and he was 40 at the time. There was a large measure of homemade equipment in all expeditions, not in the boots of course, but in things like hand knitted very fine cashmere sweaters, of which there would have been several underneath the Norfolk jacket, hand knitted woollen socks and, from pictures of Norton in 1924, lovingly knitted very long woollen scarves.

Until the Second World War most of the camping would have been done by upper-class families usually with Army connections or by the Scouts and Guides. Only the advent of the Second World War, producing the social revolution whereby ordinary working people were given paid holidays, did we see the expansion in the many outdoor activities that today we all take for granted.

One of the spin-offs from World War II was that suddenly, because of the War, it was respectable to bake bread at home, to make jam at home, to grow one's own vegetables and to make things like clothing and a tent or knit socks and so on. Many of these home arts would have been lost but for the War and luckily for us they have been kept going to produce what we now know as Cottage Industries. The coming of paid holidays for everybody has seen this boom in the manufacture of equipment for outdoor activities so that we will find in any small town throughout the land one or two shops just selling equipment for these activities whether it be walking, climbing or sailing. Why then, with this vast stock of readily available equipment, should we think it necessary to make some at home? Perhaps we can summarise why with three 's'.

Saving

First, we can save money which we can then usefully spend on pieces of equipment like boots or a boat or something that cannot be made at home.

Sizing

We can make things to our own measurements as, if you happen to be 6'8" it is not easy to buy a sleeping bag or if you happen to have a 50" waist, it is impossible to buy an anorak and a pair of overtrousers.

Satisfaction

The creative satisfaction of having made something for yourself which you can wear outdoors on the hills or sailing, especially if it brings favourable comments from your friends, is more than worth the effort that you have put into the project.

The making of a decent heavyweight waterproof jacket and trousers must still be the prime object of our exercise in making equipment. I never cease to be amazed when talking to people who have been on holiday in the Lakes or Scotland or South Wales in the summer and say "We were out walking and we got wet through because it rained". It can rain any day of the year in Britain, we do not have a dry or wet season, we have rain roughly spread throughout the year. Therefore, even if it is a bright sunny day when you start off to climb the hills there is a good chance that before you get back you are likely to need a waterproof. Of course the provision of good footwear is equally important but we cannot deal with that aspect in this book, except to say that any decent lace-up is adequate in the early stages of training but eventually, for a Gold Award Expedition, you must have a decent pair of boots that will cope with the rugged country you are going to meet.

I consider that a good weather-proof tent is the second ingredient of any good expeditioning wherever you are in the world. This shelter is not only physical, protecting you from the elements, but also psychological that you have this haven where you can change, wash, cook and eat in comfort.

A decent stove goes along, in companion, with a tent. Having adequate, nourishing and tasty food is a necessity for every well-planned expedition, but I do not recommend that we make stoves, except for the most primitive of survival stove, which would be a metal tin containing some fire-making tablets, to use in an emergency.

The fourth piece of equipment that everybody you meet on the hills would have is a rucksac and the comfort of having a good rucksac is an obvious necessity. One truism about rucksacs is that no matter how big or how small your rucksac is you will always manage to fill it with something. Therefore, to not overburden yourself you really need two rucksacs; a small one as a day sac and a bigger one if you are going on a more serious expedition for the Gold Award.

Number five must surely be a good warm sleeping bag. It is very rare that you are going to be too warm at night and, therefore, a really warm sleeping bag combined with some sort of foam sleeping mat is a necessity for a restful night's sleep.

After all these essential items there are still many things that you can design and make at home that transform expeditions from a necessary evil into a pleasant experience.

Finally, I am convinced that anyone who has been involved in designing and making clothes and equipment for use in the outdoors is always a safer person when he or she is outdoors. They have been made aware of different materials, the design and quality of making, and so have a much finer appreciation of any problems that may arise, and I have always found most people involved in the making of equipment are much more ready to repair items that might break when out in the field.

So I hope that by the end of this book, even if you have no previous experience, you will see quite clearly that it is possible for you to design and make, and even test, a wide variety of items of clothing and equipment and the quality of these items can easily match, and sometimes excel, the quality of ready-made items.

Chapter 2

MATERIALS

It is not essential to read this chapter of the book in order to produce the items of clothing and equipment described in the next two chapters. However, it is common sense that, in order to select materials for garments, tents, and the like, and then to sew them into items of equipment, a little knowledge of different fabrics, sewing threads etc is really essential. But first I would like to just transgress for a few moments into another favourite topic of mine, which is the history of protective clothing, and just look at how primitive man used to make clothes, dress himself and make shelter, just as thousands of people living today in Third World countries do all the time. When we go out on an expedition we are in effect putting ourselves into the environment that primitive people live in, in that we go to wild places, have to live outdoors and live in a portable shelter called a tent.

■ HISTORY

Primitive man, with his seeing, inventive brain, must have soon realised that the wearing of some protective garment was essential for his survival. We think that after painting his naked body with clay or woad the first item of clothing worn by the men of the tribe was a small apron. Man must have quickly realised that the wearing of animal skins enabled him to go and live in climates which were too cold to inhabit in the naked state. The creative brain again soon showed man that he could use natural materials like bark and grass to weave different items. Very quickly he must have developed the technology of true weaving because we have evidence of woven fabrics from silk and even from spiders webs coming from graves 2,000 to 3,000 years B.C. in China. However, in Britain in the Middle Ages it would have been a symbol of extreme wealth to wear a woven fabric jacket or other pieces of clothing as the ordinary people would wear felted fabrics, not woven fabrics, because of the cost.

Until recent times, waterproof clothing was provided by rather thick, heavy woven woollen materials and until the '60s the British Army relied exclusively on the British Army Great Coat as the only outer garment for winter and summer and very effective it was too. You could walk all day in pouring rain in a Great Coat and not get wet. However, it did get progressively heavier as the rain was absorbed and, of course, it would take a week to dry out after a really heavy downpour. But is anything really new? One of the favourite fabrics for richer people in the 16th century was a waxed fabric looking very much like the waxed jackets favoured by the "Yuppie" set of modern day. Then the navy contributed a fantastically hardwearing waterproof material that was used more for covering items and tents than for intimate clothing, known as tarpaulin, which is a corruption of tarred fabric, the tar being used by sailors to caulk wooden boats.

If we were playing Trivial Pursuits and the question came "Who is considered the father of modern waterproof materials?", I am sure that if you thought very hard you could come up with the answer. In 1823 a Scottish gentleman called Charles Mackintosh put his name into the English language by filing a patent for a garment to keep out the rain. The story is told that Mackintosh had a can of a new material coming in from the Far East which was rubber latex. He spilled this, much to the annoyance of his mother, on a stone slab in the cellar. Next day he found it had dried producing a very thin sheet of rubber which he could stick onto a heavy-duty cotton fabric, creating a totally waterproof garment. About the same time, steam trains were being used by ordinary people and carriages were being enclosed to keep out the weather. The newspapers of the day are full of stories that on wet days people were physically sick in the carriage of a train because of the terrible smell of early rubber, and the medical profession considered it to be dangerous wearing a layer of rubber as this would stop the "pores" breathing.

NATURAL FIBRES

Until the Second World War all the fibres used to make fabrics were from natural sources. Wool and Silk from animals and Cotton and Linen from plants. A few fibres were made from the cellulose of trees rather like the process used to make paper.

Animal fibres

From animals we would find wool, which is the most common animal fibre, but there were many more that, like wool, are still used. Silk would be the best known in the Western World. Silk is the only natural fibre that is in one continuous filament. The fibre is spun by the silkworm very much like the modern fibres that are man-made. Wool only truly means the hair fibres from a sheep but the word is often used to describe other similar fibres.

Wool

The wool industry was established in Britain when Caesar arrived in 55 B.C. and Britain has led the world since in producing fine woollen fabrics.

There are many types of wool but perhaps we only need to know "lambs" wool for our purpose. Wool is a wonderful fibre, which is springy, very absorbent and nice to wear, therefore it does not need all the half truths put out by bad advertising – like for example "Warm when wet". No fabric is warm when wet.

As with all things, wool has some disadvantages:

(1) As it is a protein it provides a good meal for some insects – moths and beetles. They simply eat the fibres and so cause holes in the fabric.

(2) Each fibre is covered in scales which point one way – so when you wash a woollen product and use too much mechanical scrubbing or rubbing the wool fibres can only move one way and we get felting or shrinking.

Of course, in the old days, everyone had "moth-balls" in the wardrobe to fend off moths and the smell of naphthalene was common at weddings or funerals when everyone had on their best suit. The phrase "out of moth-balls" has become part of the English language.

Other Animal Fibres

Mohair – is in common use in men's suiting and comes from an Angora goat in Turkey, USA etc. Fabric from goat hair is the basis of the "BLACK TENT" used by nomads throughout Asia.

Cashmere – is a very fine, soft fibre combed from the Tibetan cashmere goat and common in knitting wool.

Felting – is the production of a wool fabric by deliberate mechanical action. Felt was the most used fabric by poor people in the Middle Ages. It is still used for some purposes. Felt hats are still made.

Labels

Unfortunately there are unscrupulous people in all walks of life and textiles are no exception. A fabric may be labelled "Pure Wool" but still be made from a mixture of wool and less desirable fibres. Therefore the wool is "pure wool" but the label does not say 100% wool.

Recovered Wool is often used to dilute new wool – recovered from old fabrics and, of course, not so desirable.

Extract Wool – is recovered from UNION fabrics of wool and cotton. The process is cheap because dilute acid dissolves the cotton but not the wool.

Slipe-Wool or **Mazamet** is a type of wool not familiar to most people but used extensively to dilute new wool. This fibre comes from the abbatoir where the fibres are removed from the pelts of slaughtered sheep. The hide for leather is the main product. The wool fibres are coarse and inferior to "clipped" wool.

So you must have a label which states 100% VIRGIN WOOL and this is sponsored by the industry.

Of course there are now very many mixtures of man-made fibres and wool which will be stated on the label and these are often superior to pure wool for some purposes. Personally, I prefer a terylene/wool mixture for a suit to a 100% wool fabric.

Plant Fibres

Although probably the first garments were animal skins, the use
of plant fibres must have been very early in the development of
man. Many plants provide fibres easily.

Bast Fibres

The bast fibres form bundles that keep plants erect but have to be
separated to produce fibres. Mostly producing strong but coarse
fibres, they have many uses outside clothing, for example ropes,
mats etc.

Flax-Linen

The most used bast fibre is flax which is processed to produce
linen, samples have been found in mummy cloths 4,500 years old.
The beautiful white crisp fabric that can be produced has always
been prized, especially in the tropics, and has always had a
religious connection. The use of linen has increased with the
development of man-made fibres because of the blending of linen
and especially terylene. Terylene-linen mixtures produce a strong,
crisp, absorbent fabric that has a better crease resistance than
100% linen. Jute and hemp are two other bast fibres.

Leaf Fibres

Not much used in clothing, leaf fibres (for example sisal) are rather stiff and used in mats etc. Perhaps raffia is the only one you would recognise.

Seed Fibres

Plants often produce seeds with hairs which, like all plant fibres, are made from cellulose. Cellulose is nature's equivalent of our plastics as it is a very long chain of similar building blocks which are, in fact, glucose. For those interested in chemistry it is from glucose units that cellulose is made. The units are $(C_6H_{10}O_5)$ n; n is the number of times this block is repeated. This number is very large.

Cotton

Cotton may have been used even before linen as there is evidence of cotton as far back as 12,000 B.C. However linen was the popular fabric of ancient Egypt. India is the true cradle of the cotton industry and cotton only returned to Egypt in modern times.

Cotton is the back-bone of the textile industry. It must bear the burden of responsibility for the American slave trade because slaves were brought in to pick the cotton.

The cotton fibre is a hollow, flat tape with many convolutions. The best cotton that has the longest and finest fibres is grown in the West Indies on the island of Montserrat and called Sea Island Cotton.

The cotton fibres are pure cellulose which are highly absorbent to water but the fibres are much stiffer than wool – so we get the crisp, cool feel of a cotton shirt.

REGENERATED FIBRES

In 1664, Robert Hooke, who was a famous English scientist, suggested that we should imitate a silkworm and force a liquid through a tiny hole which, when it set, produced a silk fibre. 200 years were to pass before anyone took up Hooke's suggestion. In 1842 an English weaver named Schwabe made glass fibres.

In 1846 a scientist called Schouber added nitric acid to cellulose and made TNT which became the much used explosive. He also mixed camphor with nitro-cellulose to give us the first plastic – celluloid.

Soon someone found that a needle dipped in a solution of nitro-cellulose could be drawn into a thread and a new industry was born.

Chardonnet Silk

In 1878 Count Hilaire de Chardonnet in France produced the first real commercial fibres still produced in Brazil until 1949.

1890 saw a new process that is still used today where cellulose, from various plants, e.g. trees, is dissolved in a mixture of copper sulphate and ammonia, hence the name Cuprammonium fibre. Producing fine fibres, this was the true artificial silk and is still used in underwear, linings and chiffon today.

1892 saw the development of another cellulose fibre. Cellulose was dissolved and pushed through fine jets. This produces viscose fibre which is the most important regenerated fibre. If Cuprammonium fibre is artificial silk then Viscose is artificial cotton. Not so fine but very cheap and highly absorbent. Viscose is found in every aspect of our lives from car tyres to T-shirts.

Acetate Fibres

About 1903 it was discovered that a chemical – cellulose acetate – could be made from wood, very like the earlier cellulose nitrate but not explosive and almost inflammable.

When, in 1903, it was found that cellulose acetate would dissolve in the cheap solvent acetone, a new industry was on its way.

The acetate/acetone solution produced a strong film when sprayed onto the fabrics of aircraft wings. The Drefus brothers were brought to England to spray aircraft urgently needed for World War I. When the war finished, what to do with the factory? By 1921 Celanese was being produced at Spondon, Courtaulds Ltd also made an acetate "silk". Dr Harry Thomas, who worked in the early days on research in acetates, tells me that the great problem then was the cost of the spinnerets, groups of little holes through which the solution was pushed, as they were made from platinum and worth thousands of pounds. They all had to be locked in a safe each night. Eventually ceramics replaced platinum.

Acetates were different, no longer pure cellulose but changed chemically. Not quite so absorbent but beautiful, smooth, cheap and very silk like. One problem – the dyes for cotton that could be used on the viscose and cuprammonium fibres would not take on acetate. Much time and effort was put into the chemical research by big firms like Courtaulds to manufacture new dyes. This was achieved and acetates swept into the textile world. For example 99% of the lining of all coats and jackets would be an acetate fabric.

This dye-stuff research had a spin-off beyond the dreams of research workers in the 1920's. When in 1938 Nylon was marketed, the major success of this wonder fibre was in a large part due to the "luck" that the acetate dye-stuffs could be used to dye the nylon.

Here was a "man-made" fibre – well it was cheating a little to use natural grown cellulose. The first thermoplastic fibre that would soften and melt if the iron was too hot. Although you must remember that then irons at home were heated in front of the fire and not kept at constant temperature.

In the 20's and 30's huge quantities of these regenerated fibres were manufactured and are still used today when we know them as rayon, viscose, acetate or similar words.

MANMADE FIBRES

After the First World War the American firm of Du Pont had
such enormous financial reserves that the American government
told them to use some of the money in research. They built a huge
complex of research laboratories looking at the new materials that
had been discovered many years before which could be made into
various items which we later called plastics. Someone had the
foresight to engage an unknown Professor of Chemistry called
Wallace H. Carothers who set about looking at these new
materials called Polymers. Again the story, somewhat
romantically, is told that about 1928 Carothers produced this
material which could be melted in a test tube and then, by
dipping a glass rod into the melt, pulled out a long thin fibre
which had obvious potential as a textile material. However, it was
not until October 1938 that the commercial world was told of this
wonderful new material and it was launched fully into
manufacture. The material was Polyhexamethylene-adipamide
which none of you will have heard of but will know it under its
name of nylon. Suddenly the world had a new wonder material
that was going to transform all our lives. Being British it is rather
nice to note that the second manmade fibre in the world was
discovered in 1941, not in this multi-million dollar complex of
Du Pont's but in a rather scruffy back street of Manchester in a
laboratory owned by the Calico Printers Association. Two
Englishmen called Dixon and Witfield discovered Polyethylene
Terephthalate which you will know and is used extensively as
Terylene or Dacron. Reading contemporary newspapers and
articles it is obvious that the Americans were rather peeved that
two men had the impudence in a scruffy back street laboratory to
produce a fibre of this quality.

Of course from these early beginnings we have seen the boom in
manmade fibres so that there are now at least a thousand
chemically different manmade fibres sold in the world and if
taken alphabetically could start with A for acetate and finish with
Z for zytel. There are many more chemicals known in the world
that could be used to make fabrics but, as it costs millions of
pounds to launch a new fibre, only one or two are ever made
commercially available.

The luck that Carothers had in choosing nylon was that when the fibres emerged he could use the existing dyes that had been invented for rayon and various other fibres in order to dye and produce the brilliant colours necessary for any fibre that is to be used in the clothing world.

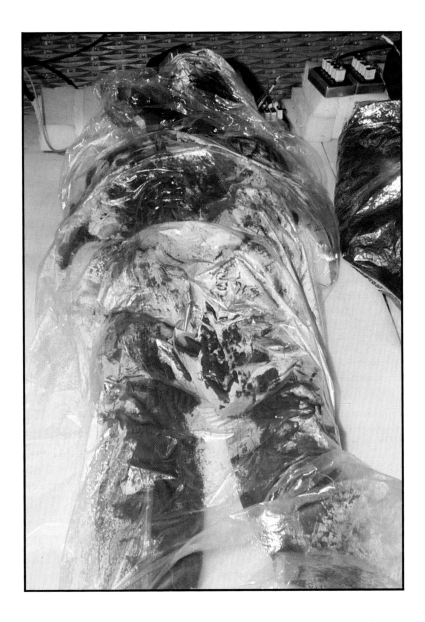

As with many areas of modern technology, people now look systematically for new chemicals to make into fibres or plastics. Two examples of that we have seen in recent times are by taking an ordinary nylon molecule and inserting another bit of molecule, one can make nylon inflammable. The fibre worn by all racing drivers in the world is known as Nomex. Then by changing the molecule slightly again we have the more modern fibre called Kevlar which is not only flame-proof but is so strong that it can be built into bullet-proof jackets.

To illustrate the strength of Kevlar, if you take one strand of nylon 1 Denier thick and 1 strand of stainless steel 1 Denier thick we see that, when we hang 6 gms on the nylon it breaks, 7 gms on the steel it breaks. The 1 Denier of Kevlar needs about 27 gms to break it.

Kevlar was really designed to go in car tyres but proved rather expensive. For special uses it has no equal, especially in bullet-proof jackets. Where helmets for soldiers were once made from Hatfield Steel the best protection is now with Kevlar fabric bonded with resin – these modern-day helmets are thicker than the steel but much lighter for the same amount of protection. Olympic canoes once made from wood, then the wonder material glass-fibre and resin are now replaced by the new wonder material Kevlar and resin.

Kevlar has one property that excludes it from climbing ropes – nylon has a stretch of 16% in the length before it breaks – Kevlar has no stretch at break. One of the latest uses of Kevlar is in the make up of sails for expensive ocean going racing yachts. The modern sails are not really fabric at all but a scrim (bandage like) of Kevlar sandwiched between 2 layers of a very thin plastic film, usually Mylar.

▇ WATERPROOF FABRICS

We are largely going to be dealing with waterproof fabrics and there are three words that one should know. The first is water-repellent, then shower-proof and finally waterproof. There are British Standards that cover these three types of fabric. There are two other words dealing with the effect of water on clothing. That is wetsuit and drysuit, but these are better dealt with in the notes on materials for insulating clothing.

Without going into the, somewhat boring, detailed account of the British Standards for the three levels of water-proofness, let us just take a common-sense definition of the three words above.

Water-Repellent

Almost any fabric used outdoors in Northern Europe that is not near the skin should be water-repellent. For example, the cover of a sleeping bag which gets drips of condensation when you are sleeping in a tent does not want to absorb that water but should have a water-repellent finish so that the drips of water run off onto the ground sheet. If a piece of fabric is held at quite a steep angle and water put onto it from a watering can it is obvious whether the fabric is water-repellent or not and this more or less simulates the British Standards test. You have all seen this effect on a car that has been waxed where the water stays in large drops. A fabric can be made to repel water in a similar manner.

Shower-Proof

This represents the next step along the stage to full waterproofness. The terylene cotton gaberdine that you buy in clothing stores will be shower-proofed at least and will stop a modest shower of rain from reaching your skin for 30 or 40 minutes while you shop and might even keep out a heavy shower of rain for a few minutes.

Waterproof

A garment described as waterproof should keep out very heavy rain for several hours. In other words, if one is walking all day on the hills or sailing in extremely bad weather, the garment should keep the wearer dry. As we will see it is not only the fabric that we have to consider but also the design of the garment and the quality of the seams (which will be dealt with in a later chapter).

To properly carry out the British Standards tests for both shower-proof and waterproof materials requires expensive equipment but, if you have an interest in this side of the technology, you will see in a later chapter that a simple device can be made at home whereby the British Standard test can be almost carried out on a simple inexpensive piece of equipment.

■ WATERPROOF COATING ■ MATERIALS

Since the invention by Mr Mackintosh of a rubber-coated fabric, modern technology has advanced somewhat and it is now comparatively simple to put a waterproof coating onto even very light-weight fabrics. Unfortunately, it has meant the massive expansion of technology so that there are numerous highly technical words used to describe waterproof garments. Let us just look at one or two of the common proofings so that at least you will have some knowledge if you go to buy fabric or even if you go and buy a waterproof jacket. The decision by a manufacturer which fabric or type of fabric he would use is a complex mixture of tradition and technology depending on cost, weight of garment, or whether it is a garment or a tent and so on. For those interested in that technology it is summarised in the table in the text.

New Fabrics: Waxed-Cotton

This fabric is exactly as it is described. It is a close woven cotton fabric which is passed at high speed through a vat of hot melted wax and the surplus wax removed at the other side. This type of fabric has been used for many years by those who either work in the outdoors, like farm workers or gamekeepers, or by those who go occasionally into muddy environments like motorcycle scramblers or trialists. A sudden increase in the sales of waxed-cotton jackets to the Yuppie fraternity is a combination of change in design and a change in technology to produce lighter-weight and better quality fabrics. The great disadvantage is that they are rather dirty fabrics and if you sit regularly in a car, for example, you will find that you are leaving behind some of the wax. On the other hand it is about the only waterproof fabric that can be truly reproofed at home by putting on an extra layer of wax. My family say that the image I project when wearing my waxed-cotton jacket exactly suits my general temperament – it is scruffy!

Poly Vinyl Chloride (PVC)

Some of the earliest waterproof garments in modern times were made by coating cotton fabric with a rather thick layer of PVC. These were worn by yachtsmen, motorcyclists and the like and were very waterproof but, unfortunately, heavy fabrics and

became rather stiff when cold. But they are still worn by some people because they are cheap and enduring in quality. These fabrics had the PVC coating on the outside but modern technology has produced different qualities of PVC so that it is possible now to use a rather thin coating on the inside of nylon or cotton fabrics to produce a lighterweight but still very waterproof fabric. One huge bonus with PVC fabrics is the ease with which seams, after sewing, can be made waterproof by welding (or glueing if you are doing it at home). PVC fabrics have large sales into areas other than clothing. Ground sheets for tents, tarpaulins, boats and canoes are just a few examples.

Polyurethane (PU)

Polyurethane is still probably the widest used material for coating fabrics. It's great advantage is that one could coat a very lightweight fabric with polyurethane to produce quite a reasonable waterproof, but still lightweight, fabric. The disadvantages of polyurethane as it is used is that there is such a small amount put on the base fabric that it is easily worn away and secondly polyurethane does not like adhesives so it is difficult to proof the seams.

Neoprene

Neoprene, when applied to fabrics looks rather like rubber and in fact one could say that it is a synthetic equivalent of natural rubber. Neoprene coated fabrics, although somewhat heavier than polyurethane coated fabrics, produces a very dense coating which is very waterproof and also endures hard wear. Because of its chemistry it is also very easy to stick tape onto the seams of neoprene proofed garments in order to waterproof them.

Most people are familiar with the skin-tight wet suits worn by divers, sail-boarders and others who go into cold water. This material is a layer of foamed neoprene, usually with stretch fabric bonded to each side to improve the wear properties – and to add glamour of course.

Silicone Elastomer Proofing

Silicone elastomer proofings will not be found in garments but in the flysheet of tents or even the covering of sleeping bags. They have been developed in order to keep the tear strength of the base fabrics.

Silicone elastomers are fairly recent additions to the proofing scene and they are materials that are stretchy. When they are applied to a fabric and you try to tear it, the proofing stretches with the fabric. PU and neoprene proofings do not stretch but hold the yarns in a fabric so that the fabric is much easier to tear.

The tear strength of fabrics drops to half the value after they are proofed with PU, neoprene and other conventional proofings. Fabrics proofed with silicone elastomers will only lose 10–15% of the original tear strength.

BREATHABILITY

This has become the most contentious word in dealing with waterproof garments. It has, of course, nothing to do with breathing but relates to the property of some fabrics to keep liquid water out but allow sweat produced by your body to evaporate through the fabric. You might think that it is an impossible task for the technologist to produce such a material but such materials do exist. Until recently it was quite easy to demonstrate that it was possible to have a material with these two opposing qualities. Most of our cornflakes and many other foods were wrapped in a clear plastic-like material called cellophane, which was similar to paper that is made from cellulose. Polythene has slowly replaced cellophane. If one glued together two pieces of cellophane to make a bag, filled it with water and tightly closed the neck with an elastic band, the water would stay in the bag. If the bag was hung in an ordinary room, the water would have disappeared after a couple of days although a similar bag made from polythene would retain the water almost forever. The water had not dripped out of the cellophane bag but had evaporated through the cellophane itself and it might surprise you to know that water does, in fact, also evaporate out through the polythene bag but the amount involved is minute.

It is possible to measure the breathability of polythene (and other plastics) but the apparatus must be quite sophisticated as the amount is so small.

The amount of water evaporated from a polythene bag is not significant with regard to clothing but is significant for potato crisps. If crisps are kept in polythene bags they go soggy, which is not desirable for a "crisp", so ICI make special grades of polythene to keep crisps – crisp!

All plastics have minute holes when made into sheets. When we keep water or salt solution for injection there must be no bacteria in the fluid. If these fluids are kept in plastic bags, when sterilised, there is no plastic that will stop the bacteria from your hands getting into the liquid inside the bag. All liquid for injecting is stored in 2 bags for safety.

Water-Vapour Transmission

So we have plenty of very waterproof fabrics, what about this evaporation of water through the fabric? It is quite easy to test this at home provided you have a means of weighing something accurately. Take an empty tin, glass or other waterproof container, fill it nearly to the top with water and fasten a piece of the fabric to be tested securely with glue or sticky tape, or some other method, over the top of the container. Weigh the whole thing and leave it for a day, or however long, and reweigh it. The only way it can lose weight is by the water evaporating through the fabric. Nearly all materials will lose some weight and certainly all plastic films will lose some water by evaporation because they have minute holes in the plastic that are visible only under a high powered microscope. It is not the fact that materials will evaporate water through them but how much they will evaporate. Ventile materials will evaporate about 600 gms of water per square metre of fabric in 24 hours. When modern research started looking for other fabrics this was used as the base level of water vapour permeability. Until recently we merely had waterproof garments because Ventile never really came much into the civilian world but now, with research, we have had appearing different tradenames for waterproof breathable fabrics and there are now at least twenty-five competitors in this field. I am afraid we must therefore introduce two more technical terms so that you will be able to understand the meaning of these words when you see them in the advertising literature of various manufacturers.

Micro-Porous

This refers to a sheet of plastic material into which the manufacturer has managed, by very clever means, to induce millions of very tiny holes so that to look at the material it looks like a continuous sheet but under a microscope you could see these very small holes piercing the plastic material. The function of these materials can be understood by referring to the diagram in the text. If you take a drop of water and cut it in half and throw one half away and carry on cutting the drop you have left in half, you eventually get to a point where it is not possible to cut the drop of water in half again. This is a very small droplet but it is reached eventually and is due to the physics of the liquid we call water. Micro-porous fabric is waterproof because the holes in the plastic layer are too small to allow the smallest drop of water to go through them. However, when you are wearing a garment made of these fabrics you produce sweat on the skin which turns from liquid water into water vapour which is, in fact, a gas and in which the particles are very, very small and can pass easily through the holes in the plastic material.

One manufacturer claims that the sheet of plastic used in making breathable fabric has 9 billion holes per square inch. The holes are therefore very small and are 20,000 times smaller than the

Water proof fabrics - breatheability

1 Micro-porous ("small holes") fabric X section

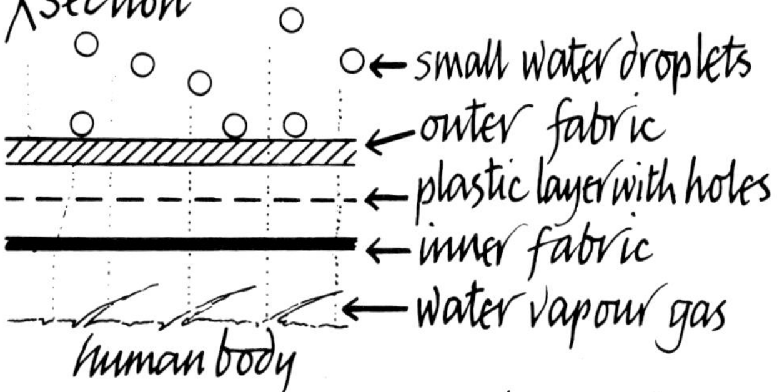

○← small water droplets
← outer fabric
← plastic layer with holes
← inner fabric
← water vapour gas
human body

inner fabric layer may be missing
water vapour is a gas with very small particles

2. Hydro-phillic ("water loving") fabric X section

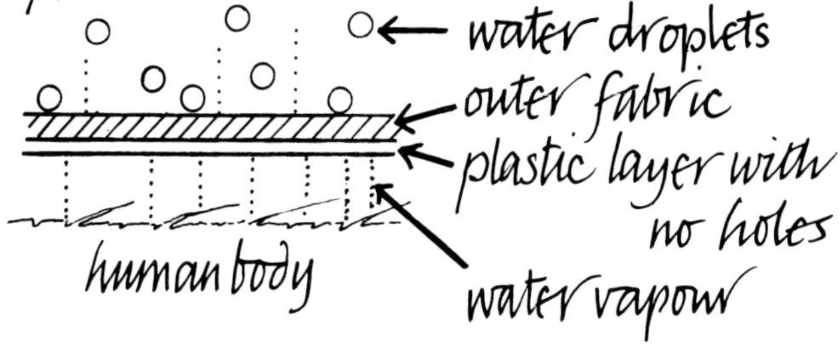

○← water droplets
← outer fabric
← plastic layer with no holes
water vapour
human body

hydro-phillic plastic absorbs water
and water evaporates through outer fabric

both types of fabric have water repellant
chemical on the outer fabric

FIG. 1

smallest droplet of water but are 700 times larger than a molecule of water in water vapour. Water droplets are about 100 microns in diameter and water vapour molecules 0.0004 microns in diameter.

I am afraid that if you have trousers made from any of the breathable fabric and you kneel on a wet surface or sit on a very wet seat, you may get water through the fabric as you have changed all the physics – rather like a cotton tent in heavy rain, when it is perfectly waterproofed until you stroke the inside with a finger.

Hydro-Phillic

Hydro-phillic means water loving, the opposite of which is hydrophobic, that is water hating. The perfect example of the hydro-phillic material is the cellophane we mentioned above where it is possible to hold water in a bag of cellophane and allow the water to evaporate through the material at a very high rate.

Unfortunately the most hydro-phillic or water loving plastic materials are either too stiff for clothing or are slowly soluble in water. Modern technology has now produced special polyurethanes that do transmit useful amounts of water vapour and are on the market under various trade names.

Leather Look-Alikes

For many years various firms did market breathable imitation leather. In more recent years some similar materials have been used for waterproof clothing and I think they are amongst the most comfortable fabrics that I have worn.

These fabrics are called Transfer Coated Fabrics when a very thin layer of foamed polyurethane is spread on special paper. The foamed material is then transferred to a fabric and bonded. When made up the garment is worn with the fabric inside. The fabrics were soft, warm and with a good feel. The comfort, I am convinced, did not come from the breathability, which was rather poor but the ability of the knitted fabric to absorb any condensation.

The most recent advance in this very complex story is the removal of the waterproof layer from the outer fabric. Most waterproof fabrics have a layer of plastic material stuck quite firmly to the outer fabric layer or, in some cases, sandwiched firmly between two layers of thin fabric. We are now beginning to get the waterproof layer, whether it is breathable or not, stuck to a very thin layer of lining material and not attached to the outer fabric at all. It is merely a waterproof lining. This is going to give the designer, especially for ski-wear, a much wider range of outer fabrics to choose from and I think we will see a big increase in this type of waterproofing in garments for outdoor wear.

KEEPING WARM

Although our main object originally in the Expedition Workshop was to make a good waterproof jacket and trousers, inevitably people wanted to make other things and one of the first things to make is a sleeping bag. So we will just have to look at fibres and fabrics associated with insulating ourselves against the cold which means some to do with garments, some to do with sleeping bags and a bit to do with hands and feet.

Still Air

Whether we are talking about a warm jacket, a warm duvet on the bed, a warm sleeping bag or, come to that, the double glazing of our houses and the insulation of our lofts, we are talking about still air. Still air is the best insulator that is commonly available to us. But moving air, of course, removes heat with it so the difference between a draughty room and a non-draughty room in the winter is pretty obvious. All the efforts we make, therefore, are in keeping a layer of air around us. The polystyrene tiles that were favourite for Do-It-Yourself (DIY) home owners to insulate and decorate ceilings, until the fire hazard was pointed out to them, gives almost the best theoretical value of insulation that one can get. This is because expanded polystyrene is 99% air. It is little bubbles of air wrapped in very thin walls of polystyrene. That is why it is such a fire hazard. The other physical fact, whatever the advertisements in the popular press tell us, insulation is largely related to the thickness of the insulator. No thin insulator will ever be as good as a thick insulator.

Fillings

What we are talking about here is having a garment or a sleeping bag with two layers of fabric and we put something between the two layers in order to keep the air still, and to keep the two layers separated by a set distance, in order to keep the heat from leaving our body. Until the advent of manmade fibres, the quality of fillings bought by rich people compared to the fillings bought by poor people was like chalk and cheese. Down, or feathers and down, is beautifully light, easily folded and very warm. The fillings bought by lesser mortals was a rather horrible fibre called kapok, a vegetable fibre that is heavy, not very warm, not very easily folded and eventually matts up so that there is very little warmth in a kapok-filled sleeping bag. Now we have a whole range of manmade fibres which are used to fill sleeping bags and duvets which approach the qualities of down.

Natural Fillings

We are all familiar with the word Down which means the small under feathers associated with water birds. A piece of down is like a baby feather without the thick and rigid quill. For hundreds of years people have been aware that using down from water birds was a fantastic means of keeping warm. People from the Far East, where they tend to keep ducks rather than hens, were firm believers in the use of down. The finest down, of course, comes from the Eider Duck who plucks the down from her body in order to line the nest to keep the eggs warm and help the eggs hatch in rather cold climates. Eider down has always been expensive because it has to be collected from the wild Eider Ducks.

This was illustrated in a story told by the actor Peter Ustinov when interviewed on a television chat show. He explained that, as a small boy emigrating from Russia to Great Britain, he did not know what was in the three wicker baskets they had brought with them. These were stored in the loft, and when the family was hard up and needed some money his grandmother would go to the loft and come down with paper bags, of he knew not what. The baskets contained Eider down and were in fact the family fortune brought from Russia and would have been worth a considerable amount of money. It is possible to buy a sleeping bag filled with Eider down, not sold in Britain as far as I am aware, but shown in the catalogue of American climbing equipment manufacturers. A single sleeping bag filled with Eider down will cost you about £1,000.

The other kinds of down come from ducks or geese and are very good for insulating, especially a sleeping bag, where you want to roll the item in order to store it in a rucksac. Even goose down or duck down is expensive unfortunately because, with the advent of duvets replacing blankets on our beds, there has become a scarcity value on these two items. However, if you have £100 to spend on a sleeping bag then it is certainly worth buying a down filled sleeping bag but not a sleeping bag with down and feathers.

However, if you frequent jumble sales, it is very well worth asking if they have any "Eider" downs for sale and you can stand and feel through the fabric to see if it is in fact a down-filled Eider down or a feather-filled Eider down because you can feel the quills of the feathers. It is quite possible, even now, to buy for £1 or so a down-filled Eider down where the cover will be absolutely filthy, of course, but inside the down will be untouched and you can either pay to have it put into a new sleeping bag outer or do-it-yourself.

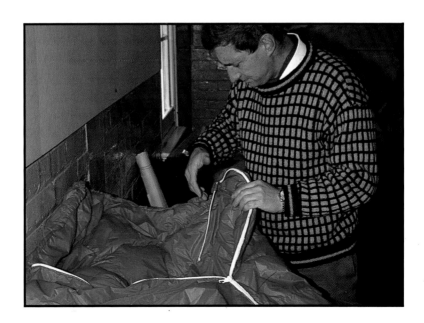

Of course the design of the sleeping bag is also important because if we just have two layers of fabric with down in between, the down will move about and you will find yourself with cold spots during the night. The easiest way to prevent the down from moving is to sew lines and join the two fabrics creating tunnels but where the sewing is there is no down and this again produces the cold spots. Some sleeping bags have been made with simple quilting like this but with two layers of quilting and the lines of sewing are staggered so that there are, in theory, no cold spots. The best configuration is to have walled quilting where little strips of fabric are sewn between the two layers of the outer fabric creating tunnels, into which the down is put. Even so if the tunnels run across your body then during the night in an old sleeping bag you find the down has settled and you have nothing on top of you only the two layers of empty walled quilting. Walled quilting is not a very ancient art apparently because at the Science Museum we managed to find a sleeping bag from the 1922 Everest Expedition which is just two layers of fabric with down put between them and of course it moved to all the wrong places. Speaking to the widow of Colonel Norton who led the 1924 Everest Expedition, who was a tall and rather thin man, she told me that her husband always grumbled about being dreadfully cold all the time he was on Everest. However, he came back from the 1924 Expedition and told her this was the first time he had been warm. And it was because somebody had suddenly had the bright idea of sewing in walled quilting but I have not been able to find out whose idea this was or who made this bag for Colonel Norton. To summarise, therefore, if you have £100, or more, it is worth having a beautiful down-filled sleeping bag but if you have less than that money you will end up with a down-filled bag which just does not have enough down in it and you will get cold spots. You will be much better to buy a good quality synthetic filled bag, or better still, make a sleeping bag yourself from fibre-pile fabric.

Synthetic Fillings

Once again modern technology has given us a whole range of new fibres to look at when thinking of filling sleeping bags. Whatever fancy names are given to these fillings do not forget that there are two main factors. One is keeping the air still and second by being springy they are keeping the two layers of the sleeping bag or garment apart so that you have this layer of still air around you. Now we have several fibres especially made for filling duvets, jackets and sleeping bags.

The change in bed coverings from the traditional wool blankets to a duvet has been extensive in Britain over the past 10 years or so. This has created such a large market for fibre filling that extensive development has produced a whole range of different fibres especially manufactured for fillings. Pillows are another huge outlet for fibre fillings.

Originally standard terylene fibres were used and are still found in the cheaper sleeping bags. Satisfactory for warmth they tend to get squashed down with use.

Now we have the "high tech" fibres claiming magical properties for example – "twice as warm as any other fibre". These claims are never borne out by non-biased measurements however, but there are some interesting developments.

Making very fine fibres does increase the insulation rate to some extent but is dearer of course. I believe one of the most important features of any filling is LOFT. This is the ability of the filling to keep springy and so keep the layers of fabric apart. Keeping the loft in use is vital as we are forever compressing the sleeping bag into a small stuff-sac.

One of the developments to give and retain good loft was to crimp fibres – like curly hair – and this has been done for many years. A new development is to extrude a fibre with two different materials side by side. On cooling one shrinks more than the other – hence curly fibres.

To increase the still air content, remember the polystyrene tiles, manufacturers have produced fibres with one or several holes down the centre of the fibres.

To summarise, there is no magical material that is much warmer than any other material. If you are going to make a sleeping bag you will have to use the materials that you have to hand. It is quite possible to make a wall quilted down-filled sleeping bag but I would not suggest that this is your first project if you have never done any sewing before. If you are going to buy a sleeping bag do not only look at the fillings, look at the covering because you are going to take the sleeping bag out into the wilds where it is liable to get torn or damaged and so on. Also demand with a sleeping bag two stuff-sacs. You want a large bag in which to keep your expensive sleeping bag during the winter, hanging up in a wardrobe or other warm dry place, and then a very small bag in which you stuff it hard to carry about in your rucksac. You do not really want to keep it stuffed down hard like that all winter.

Fibre Pile Fabrics

These fabrics are really imitation fur. They are made by knitting a backing fabric into which is blown fibres which are trapped within the knitted backing and then the height of the fibres can be controlled very accurately by cropping on the machine, rather like a lawn mower, so that you can govern the height of the pile. A whole range of different fibres exist like polished ones, curly ones, short ones, long ones or whatever because some people use these fabrics to make soft toys and various other items. The fibre pile fabrics came into being thanks to the Korean War in the 1950's when the American Government put out a message to the textile world that they were desperate for warm garments for the troops fighting in Korea where the temperatures can get down as low as − 40 degrees centigrade. A firm in America were making imitation sheepskin using this method, not for wearing but for making polishing mops to polish cars. Someone had the bright idea of using the imitation sheepskin to make a warm jacket and it was an instant winner. The fibre pile zip jacket has become standard uniform for sailors, mountaineers or hillwalkers to wear in the pub at night as a sign of belonging to this fraternity. It is quite possible to buy fibre pile fabrics on any market but I have found that they do not tend to keep the more expensive heavy-duty fibre piles that we are particularly interested in. If you are buying some fibre pile fabric hold it up to the light and in a heavy-duty good quality fibre pile you should not be able to see the daylight. There is nothing wrong in some of the lighter weight fabrics because not everybody is going to wear the jacket on Mount Everest. The other area of use for fibre pile fabrics is in making soft toys and you may well have a craft shop that specialises in this particular form of DIY and it is worth asking in this craft shop if they do have fibre pile fabrics suitable for making into garments.

Fibre-Pile Sleeping Bags

Eventually we had a new use for the fibre pile fabrics. The thick heavy-duty pile fabric which was rather too thick and heavy for jackets, was made into sleeping bags. I have found that sleeping bags made from pile fabrics are excellent. When thinking of making your own sleeping bag they are certainly very well worth looking at because it is so simple to make a super sleeping bag from these materials. We have found another great advantage of these pile fabrics is in cleaning, where if you have a child who may wet the sleeping bag in the night, which is not an uncommon occurrence, then you can take it down to the local launderette, if one is nearby, wash and spin dry it. Put it in the tumble dryer and the child will be sleeping in the bag that night. It is possible to wash or clean down-filled or fibre-filled sleeping bags but it is quite a performance and nowhere near as easy as washing a fibre pile bag.

To conclude our thoughts on keeping warm, it is not such a critical problem as keeping dry because we all have old pullovers or similar garments at home that we can take with us to wear if we are cold. Many of us now have a tracksuit that can be taken to sleep in at night or wear during the day. It might come as a surprise if some of the spectators in North Wales watching these macho rock climbers do fantastic feats of gymnastics to find that those hardened fellows during the winter often have one or more pairs of their wives tights on underneath their climbing breeches. Also in the early days of expeditions when equipment was not available many of the early Everest expeditioners had wives or girlfriends knit very thin lightweight pullovers or jumpers to wear on Everest.

Hands

Keeping hands warm is a very difficult problem because when God made our hands in four fingers and a thumb he did not expect us to go and climb mountains in the winter. However, as with other items of warm clothing, most of us would have gloves that we could take with us if we are going out in the winter. You will see from the patterns that it is fairly simple to make really super waterproof, warm mittens from scraps of material from other projects. One Junior School that I have been associated with which takes juniors skiing had a good idea of making simple waterproof outer mitts with leather scraps on the palms and the children put the mitt on over a normal woollen knitted glove.

Feet

Feet are equally difficult to keep warm in the winter but people who have been to the Poles or Everest tell you that provided your feet feel cold you do not need to be worried. It is when they do not feel cold that they are going into the dangerous condition of frostbite and you are going to lose fingers or toes. However, I think the choice of socks if you are going to go out climbing or walking or doing any outdoor activity is important and you need to wear them before you go to ensure that they are going to be comfortable. Although some people say you must only wear wool socks, some people do find synthetic socks quite acceptable and perfectly comfortable. So the answer is wear socks and the boots around home before you set off on some long journey.

VENTILE*

During World War II, many airmen were shot down and parachuted quite safely into the sea where they died from hypothermia if not rescued very quickly. Some of the early Battle of Britain pilots were provided with white chamois-leather suits in order to keep them warm if they had to parachute into the cold water. A huge effort was financed to produce a fabric that would protect these aircrew if they had to parachute into cold water. The announcement of the first fabric to meet these difficult qualities can be seen in a major article from the *Daily Express* of Tuesday 15 January 1946. The Shirley Institute, which is a Textile Research Institute in Manchester, had invented an all-cotton fabric which was eventually called Ventile, which is a corruption of the Latin for windproof. This fabric, when made into a boiler-suit with rubber neck seals and rubber socks, provided an ideal garment for aircrew and is still worn by RAF aircrew where it is known as an immersion suit. An immersion suit has to meet two stringent properties which are impossible to meet except with Ventile. First, if a pilot ditches into very cold water, the immersion suit must keep him alive for several hours when, if he was wearing normal clothing, he would be dead within say half an hour and certainly in an hour. This gives the rescue agencies a much better chance of finding the man. Many other waterproof fabrics than Ventile would meet this first property but the second property required is the most difficult one of all to meet. A pilot wearing all his flying equipment with the immersion suit over the top must be capable of doing sedentary duties for 24 hours without too much discomfort, and I am sure you appreciate that if the immersion suit was made from a plastic or other waterproof material he would not be very comfortable after 24 hours. We will discuss in a moment how Ventile achieves these two opposing properties.

I make no excuses for writing a special piece about "Ventile"*, which is a tradename. To give the fabric its technical name – close weave cotton Oxford – would not mean anything to people outside the textile industry.

*Ventile is the tradename owned by Ashton Bros.

"Ventile" is the most under exploited fabric for outdoor clothing
(and other items). It is so typical of Britain to produce a wonder
fabric and then not to develop and exploit it.

The name "Ventile" refers to a series of fabrics that are very
closely woven from very fine cotton yarns. The fabrics can vary in
weight from 4oz/sq yd up to 9oz/sq yd. They are 100% cotton and
are not coated in any way. The surface is usually treated with a
water repellent chemical – that is all.

Wind-Proof

The first quality unique to Ventile is that the closely packed fine
yarns give the fabrics a very high level of wind-proofness, i.e. the
wind needs to reach 100mph (roughly) before there is any
penetration of the fabric. The best test is described in Chapter 5
but in simple terms we clamp a piece of fabric and measure how
much air can be sucked through at a standard suction pressure.
With a gaberdine or shirting of the same weight as a Ventile you
could expect a figure of say 100, that is 100 cubic feet of air per
sq ft of fabric – with a Ventile you would have a figure of less than
1 cubic ft of air.

Waterproof

You will read in Chapter 5 that testing for waterproofness is
carried out by clamping a piece of fabric and putting water on to
the fabric. The pressure of water to pass the 2nd drop of water
through the fabric is measured.

A pressure of 100cm (39in) of water pressure must be reached to
say a fabric is waterproof. A pressure of 150cm (59in) is required
if you kneel or sit in water. A pressure of 50cm (22in) will provide
a "Shower-proof" protection. Ventile fabrics never give a result
less than 100cm and are usually over 150cm. A coated nylon
fabric will give a figure of 2,000 odd cm pressure because it has
more or less a continuous layer of plastic stuck to the fabric.

After a test where fabrics are flexed Ventile fabrics show little or
no change in the waterproof figure. Most coated fabrics show a
big drop in the figure after flexing.

Breathability

The amount of water vapour that can pass through a Ventile jacket is considerable as the fabrics are 100% cotton and are not coated in any way. In fact, when the current wave of research started to look for microporous or hydro-phillic coating, the breathability of Ventile was taken as the desirable figure to meet. I do not wish to give actual figures here because of the big discrepancies in the figures quoted for the same fabric, depending upon the particular test used.

However, let us take as examples two practical tests from my own personal experience.

The breathability is good enough to let me wear a dry suit i.e. with rubber neck, wrist and foot seals, for 24 hours doing sedentary duties without any condensation or discomfort.

Working with firemen, who wear a thick woollen serge uniform to give protection from flames, they always had one joker who, during practice would sweep a high pressure hose across his colleagues. They were instantly wet and asked for help to prevent the soaking. We lined the serge uniform with the lightest Ventile. A hose could then be played on the outside of the serge uniform and no water reached the man's shirt or body.

How Does Ventile Work?

I have worked for many years developing garments using Ventile and on experiments to explain how Ventile fabrics are waterproof and can breathe.

Some garment manufacturers and papers published from famous test houses say that Ventile is waterproof because the already tightly-packed yarns swell up when wet to fill all the spaces. THIS IS NOT TRUE.

I spent many hours wearing a Ventile dry suit, immersed in cold water, without any water getting into the suit. I can tell you that the Ventile fabric is NOT wet. The water on the surface can be brushed off.

Ventile fabric is very difficult to wet as the cotton used is unbleached and the surface has a water-repellent finish.

It is possible to wet a Ventile garment but we found that to completely wet garments made from Ventile we had to leave the garment under a cold shower FOR A WEEK.

When Ventile is wet the fibres do, indeed, swell and the fabric becomes so stiff that a jacket will stand up by itself.

Micro-Porous and Hydro-Phillic

I worked on experiments to test the functions of Ventile without success for many years and only the new wave of research into breathable fabric has produced the glimmer of an answer.

The large amounts of water vapour passed by Ventile fabrics are the function of the cellulose in the cotton fibres.

The waterproof quality is *not* due to swelling of the cotton fibres. I believe that this function is due to the invention (quite unconsciously) by the origin workers at Shirley Institute of the FIRST MICRO-POROUS WATERPROOF FABRIC. A photograph under the microscope of the surface of Ventile shows how the tight packing of the fine cotton yarns produces a mass of very small holes! Only more experiments will confirm or disprove this claim.

During World War II bleached Ventile was produced to cover
life-jackets that were filled with a vegetable fibre called Kapok.
Kapok would sink when oil penetrated the life-jacket fabric – a
common occurrence in ship wreck.

Bleached Ventile wets instantly. When life-jackets were in covered
bleached Ventile, the oil could not pass through the wet Ventile.

One of my contributions to Survival was the suggestion that
drinking water could be filtered through bleached Ventile.

The point of the story is to show how small are the "holes" in the
weave of a Ventile fabric. To test the efficiency of Ventile as a
filter we put a suspension of rice starch in the bag, the granules of
rice starch are the same size as the cysts of amœbic dysentery, If any
starch passes through the bag it is easily detected by using iodine
in the filtered water.

No starch came through the Ventile. The rice starch granules are
only 5–7 microns in diameter.

This pore size of 5–7 microns is certainly small enough to stop
liquid water – see notes on Breathability.

Bleached Ventile is also used in hospital operating theatres where
Ventile gowns filter bacteria away from the patients.

The following are the reasons for my choice of Ventile:

The waterproofness is based upon the tight weave and water-
repellent spray. I have washed my Ventile jacket many times –
and occasionally re-sprayed it.

There are no layers of plastic to delaminate or wear away.

The life of a Ventile jacket is 5–10 years.

It is a very nice fabric to wear.

THE FINAL CHOICE OF MATERIALS

Modern technology has given us an enormous world of new fibres, fabrics and finishes, with an endless range of registered trade marks but the only advice that one can give is that you must use your commonsense about these things. Feel them, try them on and decide whether you want this particular item. Just think what you are going to do with this item. Wear it, go through the bushes, scrape it on rocks and do other terrible things and think what this item will be like inside a few months. Then use your judgement to look at the quality of the sewing, the zips and other fastenings and then decide is it worth this enormous amount of money that is being asked for the item. At least when you have made the item you know the quality of sewing you have put into it. You know the quality of zip you have put into it and you will know its faults as well as its good points.

Just like the manufacturer, we are going to have to make choices of materials governed by many factors. The first of which in our case will be availability because many of the fabrics used are not available in small quantities to the general public. Then cost is an equally important factor. Most of the people I have helped have been on fairly limited budgets so that while fabric at £3 or £4 a metre is acceptable, £15 a metre becomes prohibitive to them. Then we have to consider that we are making these garments at home on an ordinary domestic sewing machine and having to finish them without the advantage of modern technology available to the manufacturer. So you will see from the table in the text (pages 244/245) that really I normally only use a very limited number of fabrics which will number about eight. With these it is possible to manufacture almost every item that you are going to need for the outdoors, except of course, footwear. I have just had to learn to be versatile and use what fabrics were available, and work within the skills of the people making the garments. However, the great factor in our favour is time as we are not going to be paying someone per hour to make up our garments. If we were a manufacturer with an order for 10,000 pairs of jeans then time would be very important to us.

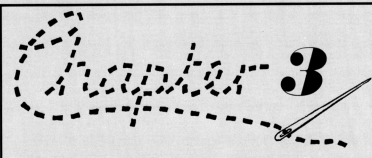

PATTERNS AND DESIGN

When in the '60s I started up the Expedition Workshops, I did
not set out to be controversial, I just wanted to teach a few kids
how to make anoraks, tents and other things. The first brick wall
we came up against was the traditional sewing teacher. I have
never had any personal grudge against any particular sewing
teacher, but I have a very strong objection to the narrow, dull
inhibited system of teaching sewing that some of them have
perpetuated in our schools. This system has ensured that
thousands of children leaving school have never put needle to
fabric again, whereas with a modern and imaginative teaching
system most of them could have learnt how to make simple clothes
for themselves and eventually run up a pair of curtains and made
clothes for their children. For example, I remember one of my
daughters coming home from school when she was about 12 years
old and saying "Daddy, today in our sewing lesson (of course
making the dull, boring old apron) the teacher took a ruler and
measured my tacking stitches and because they were not
absolutely even, I had to undo them and start again from scratch.
We then spent all afternoon hand stitching this very long hem
when in the cupboard behind us were 20 brand new electric
sewing machines."

Sizing

Most of the garments we are going to talk about, especially an
anorak, do not have to fit exactly so I am sure if you are making
anoraks for a group you will end up with a standard pattern for
small, medium, large and extra large people. But as part of the
process I have developed for the Workshops, you are going to
make and design an anorak pattern for your particular size and
shape. This is part of the whole system of pattern making in the
book and the anorak pattern you will soon be doing has been used
to make an anorak for a man of about 5 feet 10 inches but he did
have a waist of 50 inches. While at the other end of the scale I
have used it to make an anorak for my three-year-old grandson.

Anthropometrics

This is a posh scientific word for measuring people and it is
amazing how many different measurements you have to take on
any one body in order to define all the sizes and shapes that we
have to know about. Most research has been done in this field

largely for the military where they need to design cockpits, tanks etc. Most of the measurements have, therefore, been carried out on men. In recent years some of the fashion houses have realised that it may be worth knowing the size and shape of the modern woman. I do remember ringing up the Managing Director of one of the leading corset manufacturers in Britain after he had surveyed the British bust although he would not give me the full list of measurements because these had a commercial value. You will find some Anthropometric figures for Average Sizes in the Glossary.

So let us move on to make ourselves an anorak pattern.

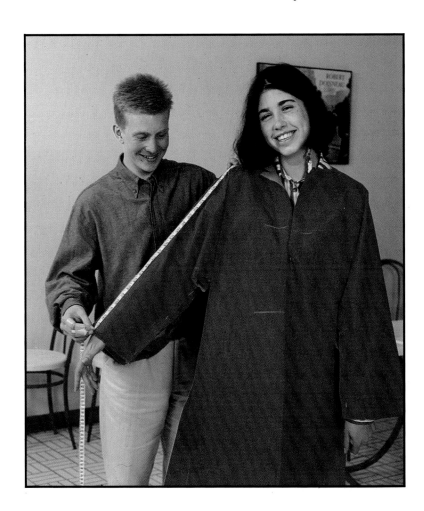

ANORAK PATTERN

Now the first heresy we are going to commit is to start with a piece of plain blank white paper and, from that, produce a pattern. If we buy a traditional paper pattern that is going to show us how to make a suit, the first thing we will notice on opening the packet is to be confronted by this mess of brown, very thin tissue type paper on which the pattern is printed. Then we will be faced with one, or sometimes several, sheets of detailed instructions in hieroglyphics that we will not be able to understand.

You see I am convinced that we remember and understand the technology that we are interested in!

Now if you turn to the page on which is printed the anorak pattern, I will go through in some detail the system of drawing out this pattern for your shape and size and, at the same time, high-light general principles that apply to making most of the other patterns contained in this chapter.

Anorak

Main piece - cut one and lay
pattern A→A along fold of fabric

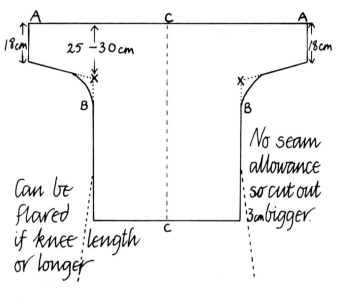

18cm

25 - 30cm

18cm

No seam
allowance
so cut out
3cm bigger.

Can be
flared
if knee length
or longer

A→A = wrist to wrist + sleeve extension
if necessary for long arms.

B→B = half of nude chest or bust
measurement plus 15cm

C→C = length from shoulder fold

Fabric width = 152 cm
Fabric required = twice C to C plus 15cm

FIG. 2

First you will need a piece of paper that is 152 cm wide (this is the width of the fabric) and about a maximum of 102 cm the other way. You will see the measurement A to A, this represents the measurement from wrist to wrist with your arms out straight at the side. Most women will find that the 152 cm width of the fabric is adequate for this measurement but many men find that they will need an A to A of 165 cm/168 cm, but we still use the width of the fabric and merely add on bits to the end of the sleeves later on and it produces a somewhat fancy designer look as though you have designed in an extra cuff. Next measure down under each A 18 cm. This represents a 36 cm sleeve pressed flat, and if you have a smallish hand you may wish to make this a bit smaller but we do this again near the end of the sewing system.

B to B represents the basic size of the anorak and you can make it to your own special size by using the formula on the drawing. This is done by taking your chest or bust measurement, adding 25 cm if you are a woman or a small man or 30 cm if you are an average size man or a large busted woman and dividing it by 2. So for a man with a 102 cm chest we add on 30 cm, that is 132 cm and divide by 2 which gives us 66 cm, so that for him B to B would be 66 cm across, that is 33 each side the centre front line.

Now we want to make the sleeve size and find the point where the sleeve joins the body of the garment. We have measured out the 33 each side of the centre line for our 102 cm man and drawn a straight line up and down to these measurements. Then along this line we measure down from the A to A line about 25 cm if you are a woman or a small man, 30 cm if you are an average man or large woman and you end up with the point marked by the cross on the diagram. With a straight edge draw from the bottom of the 18 cm sleeve line, a straight line to the cross. We get the shape of the anorak by drawing a generous curve starting 10 cm to 15 cm from the point marked X, but how do we get the other side the same shape? We simply fold over the pattern marking the centre of the pattern at the same time.

Now we must write something on the pattern that, again, goes against the traditions used in the paper pattern industry. We must mark in capitals NO SEAM ALLOWANCE on this pattern.

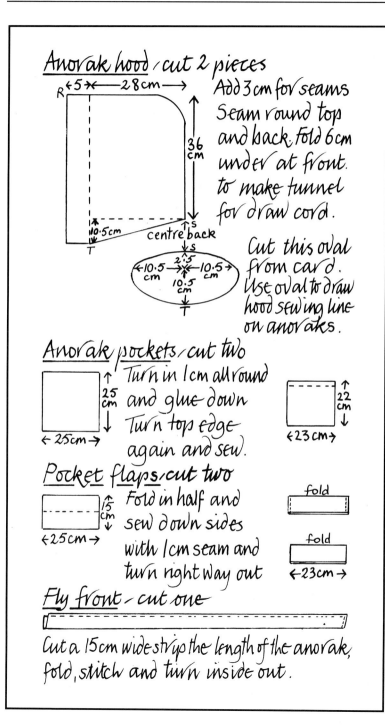

Anorak hood, cut 2 pieces

R ← 5 ↔ ← 28cm →

36 cm

10.5cm
T
↑S
centre back

Add 3 cm for seams. Seam round top and back, fold 6cm under at front. to make tunnel for draw cord.

2.5
← 10.5 cm ↔ 10.5 cm →
10.5 cm
↓S

Cut this oval from card. Use oval to draw hood sewing line on anoraks.

Anorak pockets, cut two

25 cm
← 25cm →

Turn in 1cm all round and glue down Turn top edge again and sew.

22 cm
← 23 cm →

Pocket flaps, cut two

15 cm
← 25cm →

Fold in half and sew down sides with 1cm seam and turn right way out

fold

fold
← 23cm →

Fly front - cut one

Cut a 15cm wide strip the length of the anorak, fold, stitch and turn inside out.

FIG. 3

Traditional paper patterns have the seam allowance printed on the pattern but I have found that this system of cutting out a paper pattern presenting the sewing line is a much simpler system. We are going to lie the paper pattern that we have cut out on the fabric; draw round the paper pattern so that we have a chalk line to follow when we come to sew, and then we are going to cut out the fabric 3 cm bigger all round: this becomes the seam allowance. Traditional tailoring uses this system and I am pleased to see that one of the new firms producing paper patterns for home sewing has also taken up this idea of not putting a seam allowance on the pattern.

The final measurement we need to know is C to C on the pattern. This represents the length of the garment you are going to make and is found by simply measuring from the seam line on your shoulder to whatever length you want for the garment.

So you can now cut out this paper shape which represents the basic shape to your size. The simple pattern also makes it very easy for you to work out how much the fabric and, therefore, how much the anorak, is going to cost. The fabric you require is the measurement C to C times two PLUS 15 cm. So, for example, if I am making a long anorak for myself I need an anorak of 102 cm from C to C so I would need 102 + 102 + 15 that is 220 cm of fabric, 150 cm wide. Obviously if you are making anoraks for very small people you would perhaps not use the fabric across the width but use the pattern some other way in order to make the best use of the fabric.

Hood

The next thing is to design a hood and this produces a rather large hood which I think is necessary on a garment you are going to wear outdoors when you may have a knitted bobble hat, or even a caving helmet, on.

We start with a rectangle 28 cm wide by 36 cm high. We measure down 10 cm at the front edge of this rectangle which represents the distance from your chin to your chest. Then on the front of the rectangle we add 5 cm which represents the bit you are going to turn in and sew down to produce a tunnel for the drawstring round the hood, rounding off the top righthand corner of the rightangle produces the shape of the hood.

The pockets do not really need patterns but are represented by a 25 cm × 25 cm square, with $\frac{1}{2}$ cm turned along each edge, which produces a pocket 23 cm by 23 cm, a good average size pocket. The flap of the pocket is a piece of fabric 25 cm by 15 cm folded in half and eventually sewn down each side.

Flyfront

This is a strip of material down the front of the garment that basically keeps the rain from going through the holes in the zip. You will need a length of fabric 15 cm wide by 152 cm long to make the fly. You will see from the basic anorak pattern that you have two pieces from under each arm, as it were, from which to make the hood and the pockets.

 OVERTROUSERS

I have not included precise measurements on the overtrouser pattern because there are so many variables in trouser sizing. If you look at a pair of pyjama trousers you will see they are made from 2 pieces of fabric but it is imperative that you make your overtrousers from 4 pieces because you will make a much better garment. The precise size of the four shapes indicated to suit your sizing will be obtained by borrowing a pair of overtrousers that fit you or if you cannot do this, using a pair of ordinary trousers that are a very floppy fit on you, not a tight fit like jeans. When you have selected the correct pair of trousers you simply fold them by holding the waistband at each side and pulling tight. Fold along the line of the flyzip and you will see you will have the shape indicated on the pattern. You will then be able to lie the folded trousers on a piece of paper and draw round them producing four shapes as indicated on the pattern. Do not forget to mark them NO SEAM ALLOWANCE. The four pieces will be left front, right front, left back and right back.

Salopettes or High Sailing Trousers

The easiest way to produce a pattern for these two garments is to make a trouser pattern as indicated above and add on to the waist a piece the size of the waist of the trousers as high as the underarm.

Over trousers, cut all 4 pattern pieces

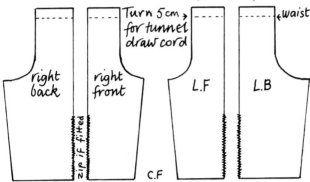

Turn 5cm
for tunnel
draw cord

←waist

right
back

right
front

L.F

L.B

zip if fitted

C.F

Get size from trousers that are a loose fit-
see instructions in text . Add 3cm for seams.
Fabric required = outside leg +8 cm (152 cm wide)
Add pockets if needed (see anorak pattern)
Add 20x20 cm patches over knees if required .
If double seat is needed use pattern above
to make shorts + put inside trousers + stitch.

Salopette or high sailing trouser

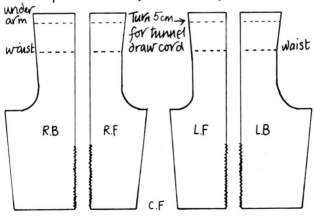

under
arm

Turn 5cm→
for tunnel
draw cord

waist

waist

R.B

R.F

L.F

L.B

C.F

FIG. 4

Over trousers for the disabled
Make up normal trousers in cheap
material. Cut down the front creases
and unpick inside leg, centre back
and centre front seams to make
4 pattern pieces.

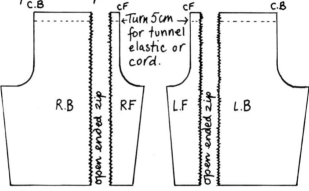

C.B   CF   CF   C.B

←Turn 5cm →
for tunnel
elastic or
cord.

R.B   open ended zip   RF   L.F   open ended zip   L.B

Extend pattern pieces for salopette
or high sailing trouser.
Fabric required = outside leg + 8cm (152cm wide)

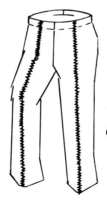

Open ended zips
down front creases.

FIG. 5

Overtrousers: Double Seat

I have found that the easiest way to make a double seat in overtrousers for those of you who sit about, or do other things, where the seat might get worn, is to make a pair of shorts using the pattern you have just used to make the original overtrousers or salopettes and inserting the shorts inside the overtrousers.

Overtrousers: Special (Disabled etc)

These special overtrousers were designed as a result of sitting on a Sports Council Committee that encouraged disabled people to go sailing, canoeing etc. We found that the reasons for disabled people not sailing were not the obvious ones, but were often reasons like access and medical reasons so that they wanted to arrive at the place for sailing already dressed. They also wanted the independence of being able to dress themselves. The main object of this design is to allow someone like a paraplegic, who is often paralysed from the waist downwards, to dress themselves by unzipping the trousers, putting them on a bed and lying on the bed when they can zip up the fronts quite easily, and thus be ready for sailing. The special overtrousers have several other advantages. They were originally made with a fibre-pile lining which was removable for washing. The fibre-pile lining kept the wearer warm and also helped to prevent the nasty bruises that can result from a days sailing if you cannot feel that you are being injured. Also we found it impossible to buy overtrousers that had legs wide enough to go over a calliper or similar medical device so that the trousers of the original models were made with very wide legs.

FIBRE-PILE JACKETS/ PULLOVER

For many years I have encouraged people to make fibre-pile jackets but have always found it a struggle myself using more traditional patterns, because inserting a sleeve is not the easiest operation in sewing. Then one weekend, I think it was in Kent, having given the basic lecture and shown people how to cut out the anorak pattern, I was amazed to find that just after an afternoons work a young lady appeared in a really beautiful fibre-pile jacket with zip and everything complete. I found afterwards that she had no previous experience of sewing, not even at school, and when I asked how she had made the jacket so quickly she said you gave us the pattern this morning and she had used the anorak pattern. Thus we arrived at the fibre-pile jacket pattern given in the book. It produces a really nice jacket which has a chunky look that fits the image of the fibre-pile fabric. You will see that you use the A to A, B to B and C to C system as the anorak pattern but slim down the basic width (that is the B to B) of the garment, because you want this garment to fit a bit closer than the anorak. The fibre-pile jacket can be fitted either with a hood or with a small stand-up collar.

FIBRE-PILE JACKET (INSET SLEEVE)

The alternative pattern given here is for the more traditional inset sleeve jacket and the only advantage of this pattern, over the previous one, is that you get a jacket that fits a bit closer to the body. I have not included a raglan sleeve pattern jacket because I have had great trouble with this style of jacket. A raglan sleeve is one where triangular pieces from the sleeve run up to the collar of the jacket and therefore affect the size of the body of the jacket. I have found with the thick fibre-pile fabrics that it is very difficult to get the accuracy of sewing necessary to produce a nice fitting garment unless you have access to an overlock sewing machine.

Fibre pile jacket or pullover
Main piece – cut one

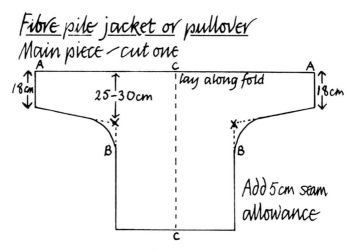

18cm ↕   25–30cm   lay along fold   18cm ↕

Add 5cm seam allowance

A→A = wrist to wrist
B→B = half of nude chest or bust + 8cm
C→C = length from shoulder fold
Fabric required = twice C to C (152cm wide)

Fibre pile jacket neck
Either hood – use anorak hood pattern
   and oval to mark neck sewing line
or stand up collar.

15cm ↕ includes 3cm seam allowance
← necksize + 10cm →

Distance around neck oval = necksize + 8cm
Cut this oval from card.
Use oval to draw collar
sewing line on jacket.

CB
2·5cm
7·6cm
CF

FIG. 6

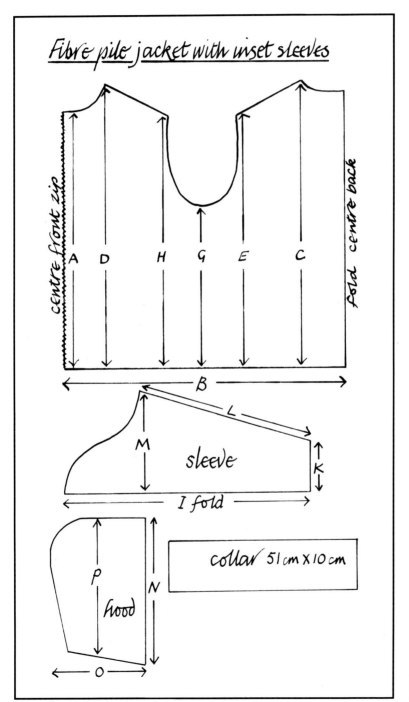

Fibre pile jacket with inset sleeves

centre front zip

A   D   H   G   E   C

fold centre back

B

L

M   sleeve   K

I fold

P

N

hood

O

collar 51 cm × 10 cm

FIG. 7

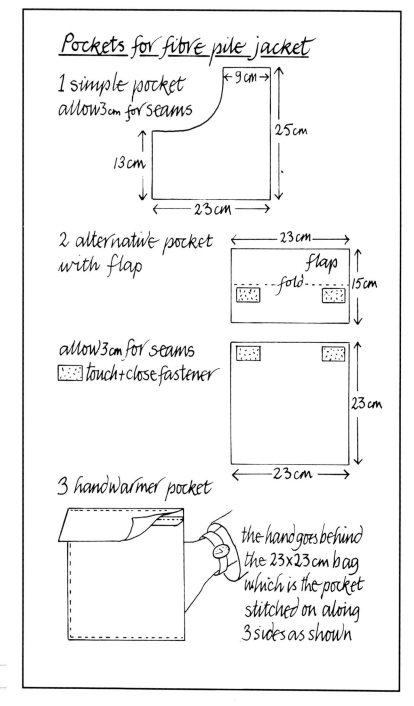

Pockets for fibre pile jacket

1 simple pocket
allow 3cm for seams

9cm

25cm

13cm

23cm

2 alternative pocket with flap

23cm

flap

fold

15cm

allow 3cm for seams
touch + close fastener

23cm

23cm

3 handwarmer pocket

the hand goes behind the 23×23cm bag which is the pocket stitched on along 3 sides as shown

FIG. 8

■ FIBRE PILE INSET SLEEVE

No Seam Allowance

ALLOW 6 cm at least for each seam
Make seams as large as possible

SIZE for Medium	Add or Subtract in cm for 1 size
A 58	3 cm
B 56	3 cm
C 69	4.5 cm
D 69	4.5 cm
E 64	3 cm
F 10	1.5 cm
G 39	3 cm
H 64	3 cm
I 64	4.5 cm
K 13	1.5 cm
L 50	4.5 cm
M 58	1.5 cm
N 89	1.5 cm
O 69	1.5 cm
P 91	1.5 cm

Collar
51 cm × 10 cm

Elastic Webbing
Measurement round hips (B) and bottom of sleeves

Zip fastener
Opened zip, spiral or medium sized toothed –
length of zip = length of jacket + width of elastic webbing
(if used).

Fibre-Pile Trousers/Salopettes

I have not included a special pattern for fibre-pile trousers and
salopettes because the overtrouser pattern given on previous pages
is quite adequate.

SHELTER

For any land-based outdoor enthusiasts there must be four or five essentials:
Waterproof anorak and trousers.
Good boots.
A warm sleeping bag.
A waterproof/windproof tent.
Reliable stove.

Of all these, the shelter provided by a good tent is perhaps one of the most important, certainly in the rather wet climate of Northern Europe. A good tent not only gives us protection against the wind and the rain but, in other parts of the world and perhaps in Scotland, the tent provides a haven against insects and other animals that we may come across in the great outdoors.

Shelter is a very physical thing but also has a great psychological factor. Very few people given a sleeping bag and told to sleep in a field would sleep in the middle of the field but would feel much safer beside a tree or beside the hedge. Sleeping in the flimsiest tent gives us a great sense of security.

Design a Tent

You will see, from the page opposite, my thoughts on shelter
which start with a polythene bag and end with a circus marquee.
I am sure somewhere between these two is a tent that will suit you
and your activities. Do not think that the circus marquee is a
complete joke as in the early '20s the Duke of the Ambruzzi, who
was a famous explorer and mountaineer, took such a marquee to
be the basecamp on one of his Himalayan expeditions. It even
had a fitted carpet!

The size and shape of tents is an endless topic and we must
remember that there are thousands of people in the world who
spend their entire lives living in a tent and that there are still
many tribes of people who are completely nomadic.

You will see from the illustrations on the page opposite some idea
of the different styles of tents that have been made. Perhaps you
would like to construct a chart similar to the one shown in the
book and award points for different types of tent according to
your own particular preference. As a result you will finish with
one tent having more marks than the others, which, in theory,
should indicate that this is the type of tent for you. Of course the
ultimate is for you to then design a new shape of tent.

BIVI TENTS/BIVI BAGS

My definition of a bivi tent is one in which you cannot sit up
easily. As the average sitting height is about 91 cm, no tent that
has a height of less than 91 cm qualifies as a true tent. This,
therefore, is only of use in emergency or for the odd night out in
good weather, unless you are a very hardened individual and do
not mind roughing it a bit.

Bivi Bag

This item is 2 metres of lightweight proof fabric 152 cm, folded
over, sewn down one edge, along the bottom and the top, then
folded over and sewn down to make a tunnel for a drawcord. It
offers no more shelter than a good polythene bag but is nicer to go

Design a tent

somewhere
in between
is the tent
for you!

FIG. 9

in to, much smaller to pack and much lighter to carry. It is also much stronger than a polythene bag and could be used in emergency as a stretcher to carry someone off a mountain. Bivi bags like this, made in the very lightweight ripstop silicone proofed fabric, will fold down and can be put into a small fabric bag about 15 cm by 8 cm by 3 cm and will only weigh about 55 gms. Thus it can be carried in the pocket of an anorak so you will always have it with you. My friend, Don Whillans, who unfortunately is no longer with us, had such a bag that I made for him when he went to climb Mount Everest. He told me that it saved his life being caught between camps when a blizzard blew up suddenly. He merely took out a simple bivi bag, still clipped to the fixed rope and went into it for 2 hours while the blizzard raged. When the blizzard stopped he came out, shook the snow off and carried on up to the next camp. Although I do not suggest that you might use your bivi bag on Everest, it would provide the same function if you were caught out on Helvellyn or some equally remote area of Britain.

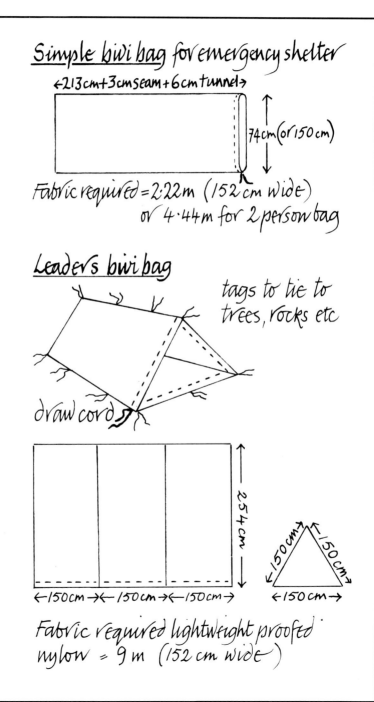

Simple biwi bag for emergency shelter

←213cm+3cm seam+6cm tunnel→

74cm (or 150cm)

Fabric required = 2·22m (152cm wide)
or 4·44m for 2 person bag

Leaders biwi bag

tags to tie to trees, rocks etc

draw cord

254cm

←150cm→←150cm→←150cm→

150cm / 150cm

←150cm→

Fabric required lightweight proofed
nylon = 9m (152cm wide)

FIG. 10

Double Bivi Bag

Another simple item to make is a Double size Bivi Bag. With 426 cm of the light weight proofed fabric, fold in half across the fabric at 213 cm, and with a seam up each side, a tunnel for the draw-cord, you have a bag 152 cm wide × 213 cm long.

A double bag is of value and I have had 3 people in my bag on more than one occasion. If you are alone the size of the bag allows you to make a tent using your rucksac as support. Modern fabrics are so light that even a double bag 152 cm × 213 cm, will weigh under 1 pound in weight.

Leaders Bivi Bag

This is the next step along the road to shelter and is an idea for a leader to carry so that if you are be-nighted without a tent or even just want to eat your sandwiches in comfort when the wind is blowing and the rain is lashing down, this item enables you all to sit together in reasonable comfort and certainly warm. No poles are necessary because you act as the poles once you are in this simple tent.

HOOPED ONE-PERSON BIVI TENT

What, in effect, we are doing here is making a rather large fabric bivi bag only we are putting little fibre glass hoops in it to make a small one man/two man tunnel tent. What the fibre glass hoops do is to hold the fabric off us so that if there is condensation it does not immediately wet you inside the tent. It is a very attractive piece of equipment to possess because you will find that you will always have it with you in your rucksac as it weighs about one pound overall. That includes poles, tent, guy-ropes and everything. If you make it in one of the lightweight proof fabrics it will cost (the price current in June 1989) about £10 overall, and such a tent sold retail but made in one of the rather posh, breathable fabrics would cost you over £100. Many people think that the three millimetre fibre glass poles suggested look rather

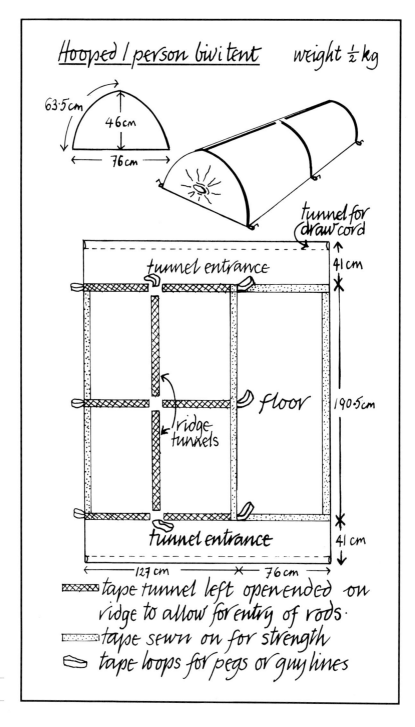

Hooped 1 person bivi tent   weight ½ kg

63.5cm
46cm
76cm

tunnel for draw cord
tunnel entrance
41cm
floor
ridge tunnels
190.5cm
tunnel entrance
41cm
127 cm   76 cm

tape tunnel left open-ended on ridge to allow for entry of rods.
tape sewn on for strength
tape loops for pegs or guy lines

FIG. 11

flimsy, but my good friend John Anderson who is a lecturer in Outdoor Education has used such a tent for several years when he walks alone on the Alps. By having a drawcord entrance at each end of the tent it gives you very good access and, although really a one person tent, two people can share it somewhat intimately by one person going in to the other end of the tent.

TWIN HEIGHT, TWO-PERSON BIVI TENT

I developed this bivi tent in response to two factors. The first that the small diameter fibre glass rods were not easy to come by, and then a good friend wanted to take his new wife to Scotland and spend the odd night in remote areas but did not want to carry a full tent. As his wife is no longer a young lady, I felt that she would not like to struggle to dress and cook in a small bivi tent. I therefore evolved the idea of taking the two 51 cm poles, putting one inside the other so one can then elevate the centre to produce a 94 cm high tent which is quite adequate for primitive cooking.

The idea of the wing is to keep the rain off the walls so that the vertical wall can be made of a non-proof material thereby eliminating the condensation normally associated with bivi tents. This shape of tent works very well and is an ideal tent for two people who only want to spend an odd night or two in the wild. I would suggest that, if you want to make a super version of this, you make up a flysheet the size and shape of the roof plus wings with four eyelet holes which will slip over the poles and this takes the force of any torrential downpour you may happen to meet. If you do not have enough fabric to do this then a polythene flysheet will be quite adequate.

An idea that you might like to try is to make a square front bivi tent in polythene. It is not difficult to make this bivi tent using say 500 gauge polythene for the roof and floor and thinner polythene for the sides and wings and it makes quite a useful little tent to carry with you in case you are caught out in bad weather. Of course the polythene will not be sewn together but stuck with say 3 inch self-adhesive tape which can be bought quite cheaply from various shops where it is sold as either carpet tape or tape for putting on packing cases. You will find that some of the camping shops and garden centres sell polythene sheets 2 metres wide, but it is possible to pick up very big polythene bags for nothing if you approach your local furniture shops because mattresses for beds come in such a size polythene bag that it is quite easy to turn it into a tent.

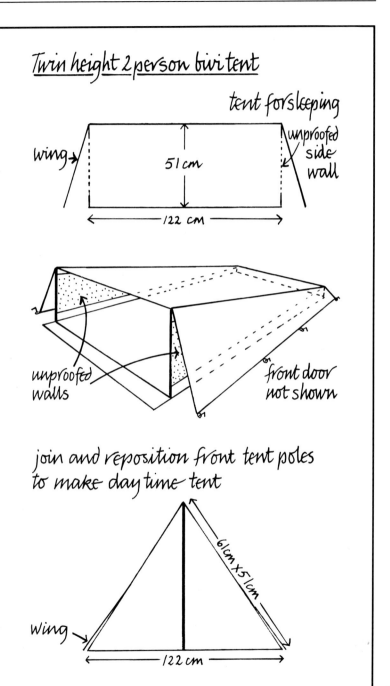

Twin height 2 person bivi tent

tent for sleeping

wing→

unproofed side wall

51 cm

122 CM

unproofed walls

front door not shown

join and reposition front tent poles to make day time tent

61 cm x 51 cm

wing →

122 cm

FIG. 12

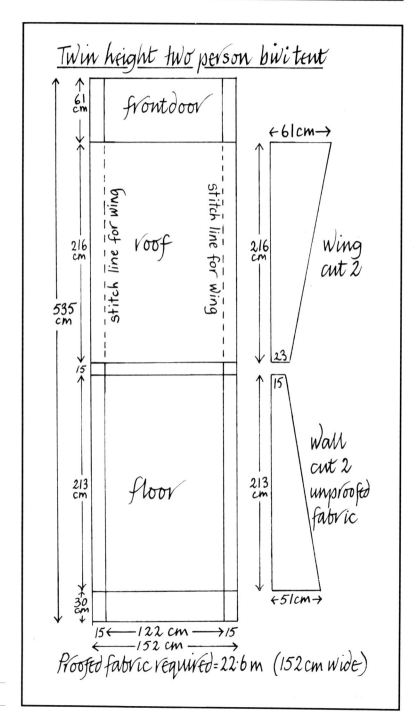

Twin height two person bivi tent

front door

roof

stitch line for wing

stitch line for wing

61 cm

216 cm

535 cm

15

213 cm

30 cm

floor

←61cm→

216 cm

23

15

213 cm

Wing
cut 2

Wall
cut 2
unproofed
fabric

←51cm→

15 ←—122 cm—→ 15

←—152 cm—→

Proofed fabric required = 22.6 m (152 cm wide)

FIG. 13

■ HOOPED TWO-PERSON BIVI TENT

You will see from the diagram that the two-man hooped tent is made to the same principles as the hooped bivi tent but just made bigger, so that we now have a tent which is 122 cm wide and a height of 99 cm. This means that it is quite easy for someone to sit in this tent which makes it quite a comfortable shelter to occupy for more than one night. You will be surprised if you make this tent, how big it seems once you have erected the whole thing and looking in it, it looks like a small marquee. What I have also added to this two-man tent is a porch at each end so that you have room to store some equipment, say rucsacs or various bits and pieces and also somewhere to do some cooking if it is a rainy, or particularly windy, day. Several manufacturers have produced tents of this general type but often have the fibre glass poles hung from a strip of fabric. I prefer to have the fibre glass rods in tight little pockets made by sewing tape onto the outer fabric because this seems to make a much stronger tent which has much less sway when it is very windy. It would be quite easy for you to alter the size of the hoops and the length of the tent if you so wish and the way to do this is to get hold of some flexible plastic tubing. I buy lengths of 1 inch plastic tube that is readily available in DIY shops and it is used for overflows on sinks. You will find it quite easy to use this flexible tube to make up a full sized hoop to the dimensions you wish to choose and then measure round the hoop to find the distance from one side to the other which will govern the size of the fabric you are going to use when you make up the tent. I have found it very difficult to work out this distance theoretically, because it is not a semi-circle but a semi-circle with straight walls for a short distance before the ground. You could alter the shape and size of the porches if you so wished and again I just set up a full size hoop using the plastic tube, and bits of string or canes, to get the shape and measurements of the porches.

The design of the two-man hooped tent shown is for a single skinned tent which obviously has problems because you can get condensation in the tent which then runs down onto the ground sheet and can wet your sleeping bag if you are not raised off the floor on a sleeping mat. It is not difficult to convert this tent

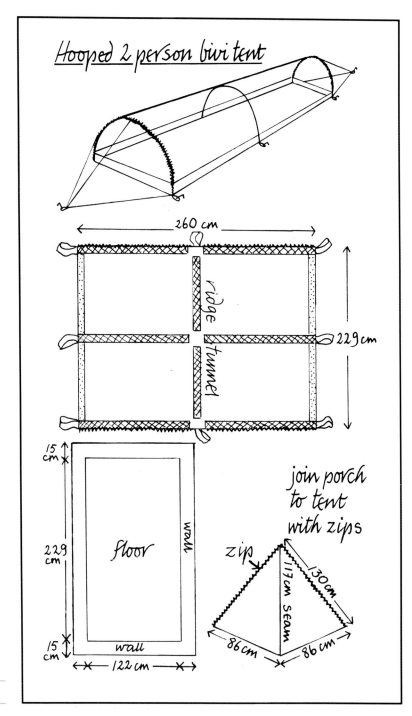

Hooped 2 person bivi tent

260 cm

ridge tunnel

229 cm

15 cm

229 cm

floor

wall

wall

15 cm

122 cm

join porch to tent with zips

zip

117 cm seam

130 cm

86 cm

86 cm

FIG. 14

into a two skinned tent which would eliminate the problems of condensation. You would make a liner from some non-proofed material to be a couple of inches smaller than the outer tent and this liner would be tied at several places to the outer tent to give it the shape. Of course the ground sheet must be attached to the inner otherwise the condensation will still run onto the floor and wet your sleeping bag. I would suggest to you if you want to make a really super high quality tent, you could attach a lightweight ground sheet to the inner tent you have made so you end up in effect with the outer waterproof tent, with the waterproof ground sheet, inside which you have the inner tent attached to another lightweight ground sheet. This I can tell you makes a very weatherproof and windproof piece of equipment.

BASIC RIDGE TENT

This pattern represents the traditional ridge tent design that was "invented" by Whymper who is famous for climbing the Matterhorn for the first time. The original Whymper tent is stored in the cellar of the Alpine Club in London. Whymper used 2 straight poles and I am not aware of the person who invented "A" poles giving a clear space for the entrance.

A ridge pole is well worth the tiny extra weight. By keeping the ridge straight, the whole tent sits better and performs better in high winds.

Designing clothing for aircrew who, when they eject from a modern jet face winds of 300–400 mph, research workers soon discovered that once a fabric flaps it will tear. Fabrics held tight will not tear so easily. So it is important that a tent is put up square and true with the flysheet held as tight as possible.

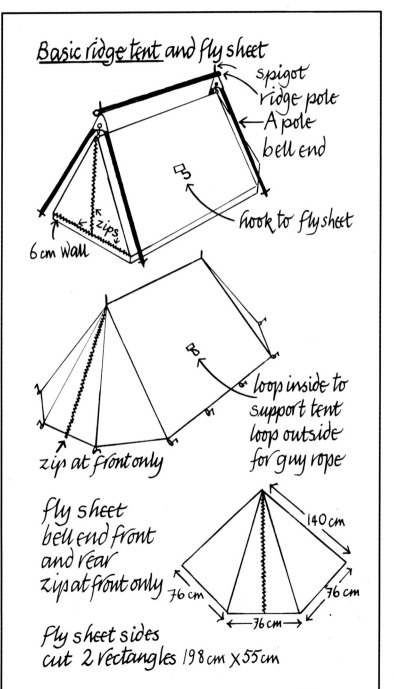

Basic ridge tent and fly sheet

spigot
ridge pole
A pole
bell end

hook to fly sheet

zips
6 cm wall

loop inside to
support tent
loop outside
for guy rope

zips at front only

fly sheet
bell end front
and rear
zips at front only

140 cm
76 cm
76 cm
76 cm

fly sheet sides
cut 2 rectangles 198 cm × 55 cm

FIG. 15

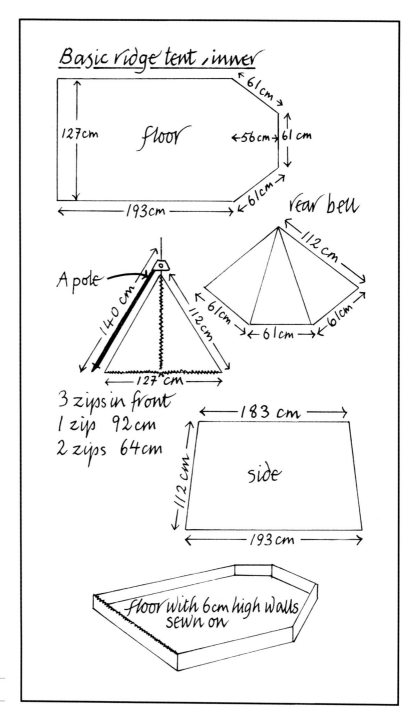

Basic ridge tent, inner

floor

127cm

193cm

61cm

56cm

61cm

61cm

61cm

A pole

140 cm

112 cm

127 cm

3 zips in front
1 zip 92 cm
2 zips 64 cm

rear bell

112 cm

61cm

61cm

61cm

side

183 cm

112 cm

193 cm

floor with 6cm high walls sewn on

FIG. 16

TRANS-RIDGE TENT

I have included the pattern for a cross-ridge tent, although I do not have any personal experience of using this design.

A trans-ridge tent is a tent where you sleep at 90 degrees to the ridge, that is across the ridge. In a traditional tent you sleep parallel to the ridge. I believe that the Tent Trade produced cross-ridge tents when the width of fabrics changed from 91 cm wide for cotton to 152 cm wide for nylon and terylene-cotton.

OTHER TENT DESIGNS

There are so many different shapes and sizes of tent that it is not possible to give you detailed designs and making instructions for every style and shape. If you wish to make some other style and type of tent, the best way is to find a friend who has a model of that particular tent and, when the tent is erected, it is not very difficult to then measure up the size and shape of each panel and adapt it to your own needs. Of course it is strictly illegal to copy someones registered design, but I am sure no one is going to prosecute you if you merely make one tent for your own use. If you have a bright idea in your mind of a new style or type of tent, then I suggest to you the best way of making it is to make small scale models from thin card, when you see the problems and you will see then the shape of each panel and so on that you will have to cut out and sew together. You will then have to work out the best way of cutting the fabric to get the best use of the areas involved because you are going to use quite a few yards of fabric. If you are going to make a special sized tent or different shaped tent, it is useful to remember that you will have to have poles to hold it and if you are not using standard sizes you may have problems in obtaining them, but you will see in the next chapter that it is possible to buy aluminium tubing and create your own poles without too much trouble.

Trans ridge tent

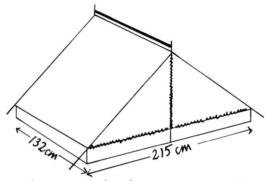

132cm

215 cm

poles   2 singlepoles 102 cm with spike
         1 ridge 132 cm
   or   2 A poles 158 cm with spike
         1 ridge 132 cm

3 zips at each end of inner tent
1 zip at each end of fly sheet
inner tent side panels two 132 cm X 142cm
fly sheet main panels two 132 cm X 198cm

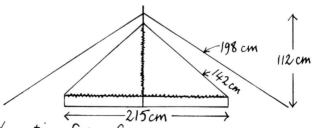

198 cm

112 cm

142 cm

215cm

X section from front
showing 102cm high tent (including 10cm high wall)
and fly sheet

FIG. 17

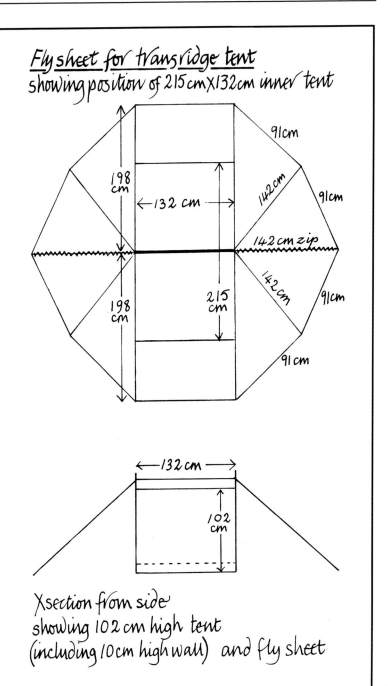

Fly sheet for transridge tent
showing position of 215 cm × 132 cm inner tent

91cm

198 cm

←132 cm→

142cm

91cm

142 cm zip

215 cm

198 cm

142cm

91cm

91 cm

←132 cm→

102 cm

X section from side
showing 102 cm high tent
(including 10 cm high wall) and fly sheet

FIG. 18

SLEEPING BAGS

When you pick up one of the monthly magazines on camping and the outdoors and see that they can review 200 different sleeping bags, it would not be possible for me to give you patterns for all the different shapes and sizes of bags that are available. Therefore I have considered two styles of bag, that is the traditional square shaped, or oblong, bag with a zip down the long side and across the bottom so it can be opened flat; and two tapered bags. The advantage of the oblong bag is that you can unzip it and use it as a quilt on a bed or, if you so wish and have two of these bags, you can zip them together to produce a double-sized sleeping bag. The disadvantages of these large bags are that you have a big bulk to warm up before you get warm and then when you move in the night, it is quite possible to hit a cold spot in the bag.

The tapered design of bag has the advantage that it is very much less bulky and when you have warmed it up and you turn over in the night you tend to turn the bag with you so you never feel these terrible cold spots that you get in the square bag. All three designs are intended to be made up in heavy duty fibre-pile fabric, which is an interesting return to an historical design, as Captain Scott used a fur sleeping bag on his fateful journey to the South Pole, but of course this was a bag from natural fur such as seal skin. I suggest to you the use of fibre-pile fabrics because it is a very simple item to make, but also a very effective means of keeping warm. A few hints on making up sleeping bags from other materials are found in the chapter on Making-Up.

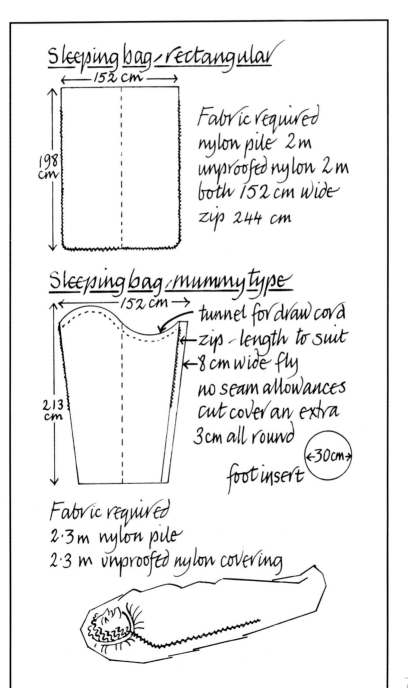

Sleeping bag - rectangular

←— 152 cm —→

198 cm

Fabric required
nylon pile 2 m
unproofed nylon 2 m
both 152 cm wide
zip 244 cm

Sleeping bag - mummy type

←— 152 cm —→

213 cm

tunnel for draw cord
zip - length to suit
8 cm wide fly
no seam allowances
cut cover an extra
3 cm all round

←30cm→

foot insert

Fabric required
2·3 m nylon pile
2·3 m unproofed nylon covering

FIG. 19

Sleeping bag · tapered with hood or collar

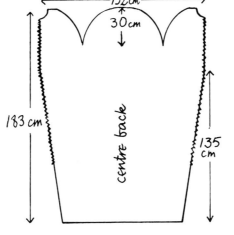

152cm

30cm

183 cm

centre back

135 cm

foot insert

30cm

No seam allowances
Fabric required — nylon pile 2·3 m
Unproofed nylon covering 2·3 m
Cut cover 3cm bigger all round
Zip — no longer than 152 cm

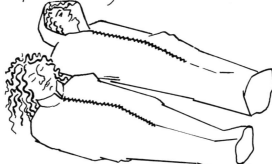

Refer to fibre pile jacket and
anorak plans for collar and hood
patterns and instructions

FIG. 20

■ RUCKSACS

I find it difficult to keep track of the number of styles and shapes, and especially colours, of rucksacs. There must be hundreds of different styles and colours and so on. From experience I can tell you one true fact about any rucksac is that no matter how big or how small your rucksac, you will always manage to fill it. So I think the keen expeditioner really needs two rucksacs: you need a daysack when you are going out for the day just to carry waterproofs, a camera, sandwiches and so on, and a big sack of some style for when you are going on a Duke of Edinburgh's Award expedition or similar adventure. Although we are dealing with a functional item, there is no doubt there is a large element of fashion in what you can buy in the shops today, not only in the colours but in the style of the sack. Until recently any large sack would be attached to a large external frame, the design of which is based upon the early wooden frames made by the expeditioners many years ago in the Canadian forests and in the Arctic countries. We have gone from this large external frame to some sort of internal support which could be a metal frame or just stiff foam which contours itself to your body and holds the weight near to your centre of gravity. However, I think it is true to say that if you are going on a long expedition and carrying a very heavy pack, then an external framed rucksac is still one of the designs that you should look at.

■ LARGE DAYSACK

The drawings give a lot of detail on the design of this fairly large daysack. However, I wish you to treat this design like the design for the anorak as a general design for any size of rucksac. You will see from the sketch that the rucksac consists of a base, back piece and a front which is tapered to give you the volume in the rucksac high up. On the design you will see the back is a piece 30 cm by 53 cm; the base is a piece 30 cm by 15 cm and the front is a piece 61 cm wide going out to 86 cm wide and between 53 cm and 69 cm long. All these measurements could be changed if you wished to make a larger or smaller rucksac, one for a very big person, or even for a child. The use of thin card models is another way of getting a design to the size and shape that you wish to make.

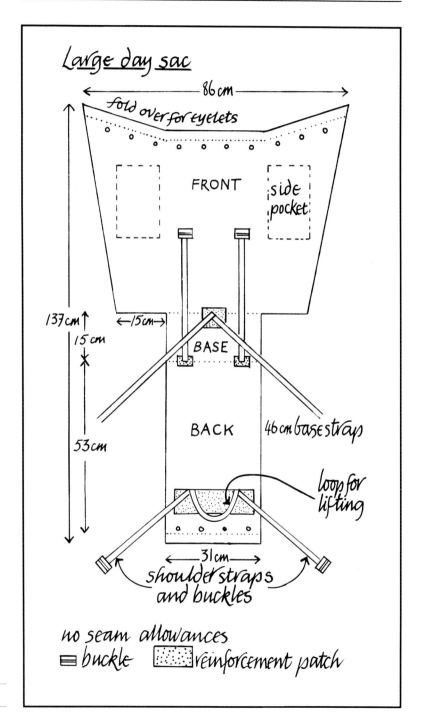

FIG. 21

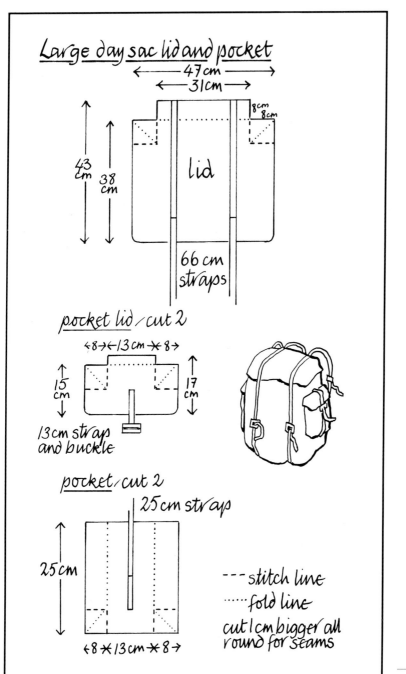

Large day sac lid and pocket

← 47cm →
← 31cm →

43 cm   38 cm   8cm 8cm

lid

66 cm straps

pocket lid / cut 2

← 8 → ← 13 cm → ← 8 →

15 cm   17 cm

13 cm strap and buckle

pocket / cut 2

25 cm strap

25 cm

← 8 → 13 cm → 8 →

--- stitch line
····· fold line
cut 1 cm bigger all round for seams

FIG. 22

ALTERNATIVE RUCKSAC

The alternative rucksac pattern has been included because it is not only a way of making a different shaped rucksac but it is a pattern that can be used without the carrying straps to make stuff sacks or camera carrying bags or other similar items. Again the measurements can be changed *ad infinitum* provided you remember that the distance round the D-shaped base must equal the length of the fabric you are going to sew to it.

Frames for Rucksacs

Over the years I have made many large rucksacs with external frames using the large day sack pattern made bigger, usually to get a very large rucksac and, if you are having an external frame, the carrying straps are attached to the frame and not the rucksac. The rucksac is usually just hung from two very strong loops onto the top of the frame and attached to the bottom of the frame by a couple of straps.

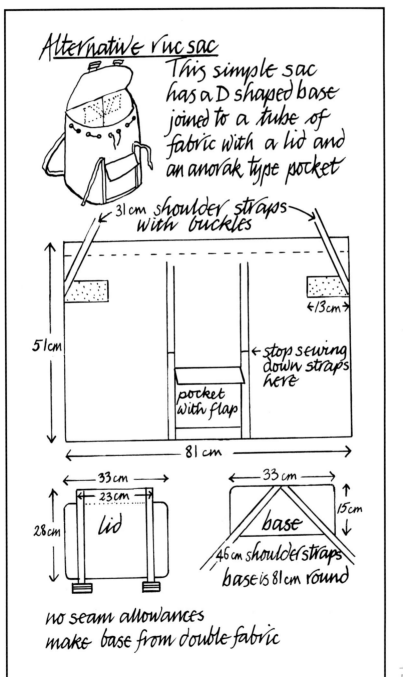

Alternative rucsac

This simple sac has a D shaped base joined to a tube of fabric with a lid and an anorak type pocket

31 cm shoulder straps with buckles

13 cm

51 cm

stop sewing down straps here

pocket with flap

81 cm

33 cm

23 cm

lid

28 cm

33 cm

15 cm

base

46 cm shoulder straps

base is 81 cm round

no seam allowances
make base from double fabric

FIG. 23

Stuff sacs for sleeping bags
Large storage sac

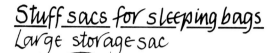

length 76 cm
diameter 33 cm
circumference 102cm

Fabric needed
86 cm (76 cm + 10 cm for tunnel and seam) wide
by 107cm (102 cm + 5cm for seams) long
base 38 cm diameter (33cm + 5cm for seams)

length 38 cm
diameter 25 cm
circumference 76cm

Fabric needed for small sac for carring out
48cm (38cm + 10 cm for tunnel and seam) wide
by 81cm (76 cm + 5 cm for seams) long
cut base and lid from fabric 30 cm × 64 cm

compression bag

stitch 4 pairs straps + buckles
into seams
draw up to reduce volume

FIG. 24

The frames are made from about 3 cm diameter aluminium tubing, which is not difficult to find, either in Do-it-Yourself shops where it is rather expensive or if you look in Yellow Pages you will find every town of any size has an aluminium stockist. The aluminium tube can be quite easily bent and for many years I just had a piece of thick old oak with a hole in it, which was held in a vice and the tube could be bent quite easily. However, eventually I acquired a pipe bender which I have found is not an unusual piece of equipment in these days of DIY plumbing. With the pipe bending machine it is of course much easier to make accurate bends and angles in the tubing.

How can we hold the aluminium tubing together? It was by chance that a colleague found that having looked at an old roofrack on the local dump, he found that the roofrack was held together by a very simple system and this is the one I have used for many years. It consists of small saucer shaped pieces of spring steel which are pushed into the aluminium tubing. A screw is pushed through a hole in the other piece of aluminium tubing and screwed into the saucer shaped metal inside the tube. When tightened up this makes a very strong resilient joint that can be taken apart if necessary. The problem is one piece of tubing has to be shaped to match the other piece of tubing, but I found that in one of the large motoring retailers it is possible to buy all these bits and pieces because they are held as spares for roofracks.

It is quite possible for you to design a new style and shape of rucksac and, again, making the models in small card will help, or if you have seen a rucksac that you like why not borrow one from a friend and copy and adapt it.

BITS AND PIECES

There are many small items that it is well worth making because all of them will cost a few pounds to buy and the few pounds you have saved by making these items can then be put into a super pair of boots or other items that you cannot make. I have included some items that are well worth making, but I hope that you will get the "making" bug and even design some items yourself just for the pleasure of creating some item that's yours.

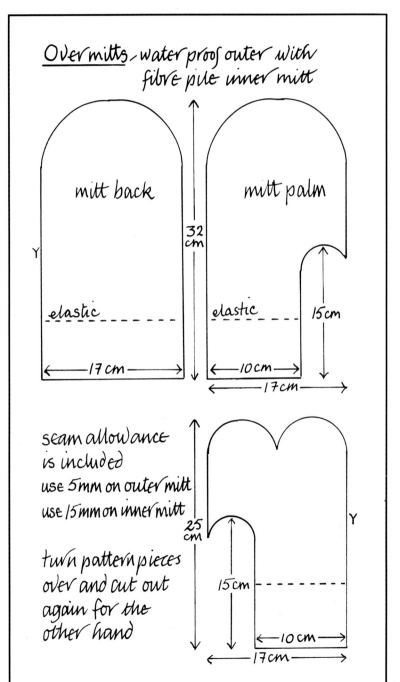

Over mitts - water proof outer with fibre pile inner mitt

mitt back

mitt palm

32 cm

Y

elastic

elastic   15 cm

←— 17 cm —→   ←— 10 cm —→

←— 17 cm —→

seam allowance
is included
use 5mm on outer mitt
use 15mm on inner mitt

25 cm

15 cm

Y

turn pattern pieces
over and cut out
again for the
other hand

15 cm

←— 10 cm —→

←— 17 cm —→

FIG. 25

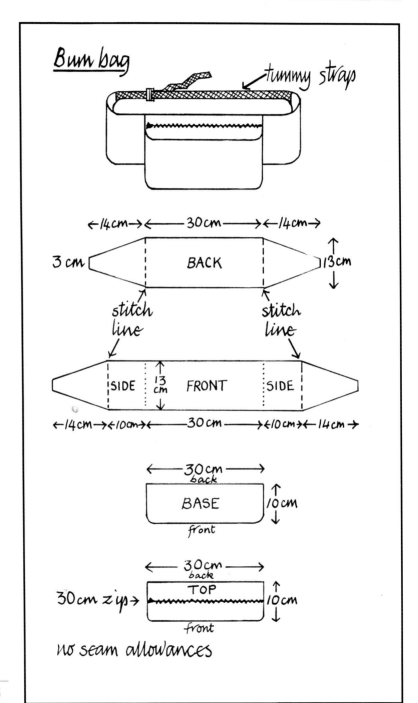

FIG. 26

GAITERS

Gaiters are one of the most simple items to make and you can use small bits of material left from other projects to make them. However, a pair of gaiters in a shop will cost you at least £10, and perhaps more, so they are well worth making because they are an essential item for the British climber. There is only one thing you need to remember when designing gaiters. A gaiter must be able to stand up by itself. Although you will have a draw cord round the top of the gaiter, there is no way that you can pull it tight enough to hold the gaiter up without cutting off the circulation of blood to your feet. So you must use stiff waterproof material from which to make the gaiters and I use the 4 plus 4 (that is 270gm) for this purpose. In order to make sure that the gaiters are stiff enough and stand up easily by themselves, I concentrate on the seam down the front of the gaiter, into which I insert two or three strands of PVC coated garden wire which is quite stiff enough to do the job.

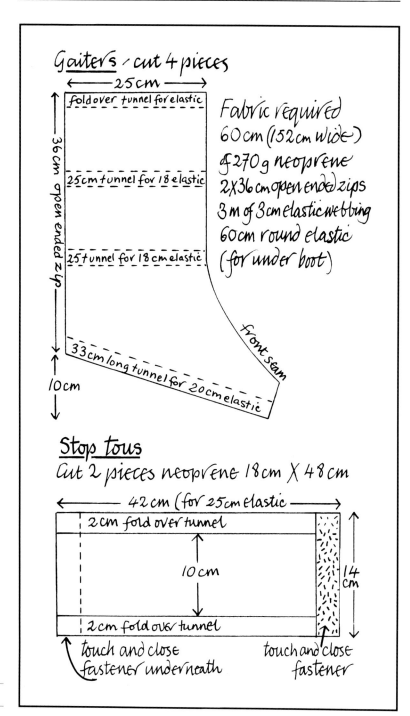

Gaiters - cut 4 pieces

←——— 25cm ———→

fold over tunnel for elastic

Fabric required
60cm (152cm wide)
of 270g neoprene
2×36cm open ended zips
3m of 3cm elastic webbing
60cm round elastic
(for under boot)

36cm open ended zip

25cm tunnel for 18 elastic

25 tunnel for 18 cm elastic

front seam

33cm long tunnel for 20cm elastic

10cm

Stop tous

Cut 2 pieces neoprene 18cm X 48cm

←——— 42cm (for 25cm elastic ———→

2cm fold over tunnel

10 cm

14 cm

2cm fold over tunnel

touch and close
fastener underneath

touch and close
fastener

FIG. 27

WATERPROOF PONCHO

Walkers in some countries swear by the poncho cape and the revival of interest in military equipment in the UK has seen the use of this item increasing.

Very simple to make from one piece of waterproof material. Measure from your shoulder seam to the required length – be generous – about 102 cm for an average person. You will need 2 times this length. You have an oblong 150 cm × (say 203 cm) which needs a strong hem all round. You can fit a hood using the instructions for the anorak hood – the oval for the hood being put in the centre of the fabric.

One advantage of the poncho cape lies in the dual use as a bivvi-sheet for shelter.

To use as a shelter the poncho requires small squares of thicker fabric, thin leather or similar material sewn at each corner and 2 or 3 places down each side. These reinforcement patches are for attaching loops of webbing.

Another useful addition is a flap of fabric sewn on to cover the "neck-hole" when you use the poncho as a bivvi-sheet.

Large Poncho

Many people make the poncho larger than the standard measurements to give enough length at the back to cover the rucksac.

To make this type you will need 2 times the length that you measured (e.g. 102 cm) plus about 38 cm. The hole for the hood is now put 102 cm from the front edge of the cape leaving 102 cm + 38 cm at the rear. If you are walking without a rucksac then the 38 cm flap at the rear can be turned under and held with touch and close tape or press studs.

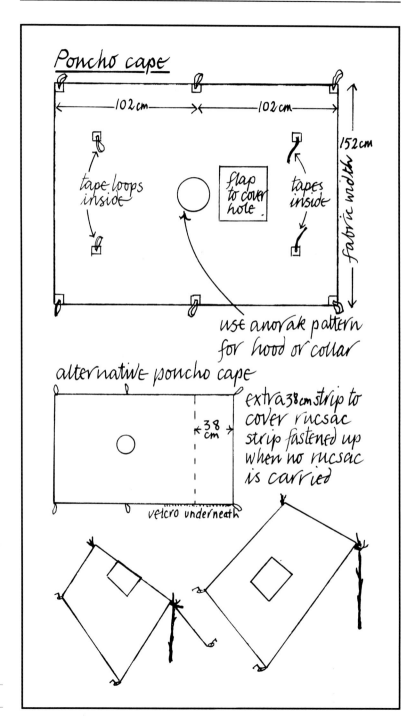

Poncho cape

102 cm — 102 cm

152 cm

fabric width

tape loops inside

flap to cover hole.

tapes inside

use anorak pattern for hood or collar

alternative poncho cape

38 cm

extra 38cm strip to cover rucsac strip fastened up when no rucsac is carried

velcro underneath

FIG. 28

RAIN-PROOF LEGGINGS

This type of waterproof leg protector was the favourite garment in the 20's and 30's when cycling was the most popular form of transport. Worn under the cape they kept the legs dry but are not so hot and sweaty as trousers.

Worn under a long anorak/jacket they are good for walking in the rain, wet grass or heather.

Cut a pattern from a pair of overtrousers or other baggy trousers. A waist belt is easily made from a piece of webbing.

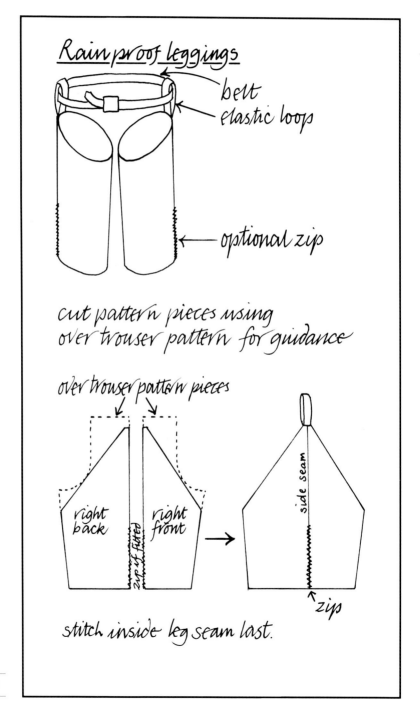

Rainproof leggings

belt
elastic loops

optional zip

cut pattern pieces using
over trouser pattern for guidance

over trouser pattern pieces

right back

right front

zip if fitted

side seam

zip

stitch inside leg seam last.

FIG. 29

CYCLIST TYPE CAPE

This style of cape was once standard uniform for cyclists. Many styles will be found in Holland where cycling is still a major form of transport. A cape is certainly worth considering for walking in some parts of the UK.

A hood can be made from the anorak hood pattern. The sizes on the pattern are for a medium sized man, but it is a simple matter to cut a pattern for your own use.

As with the poncho cape, when you are carrying a rucksac it is much more convenient to have the cape over the rucksac. So often in the UK the weather is showers with sunny intervals and if the cape (or anorak) is under the rucksac it is frustrating to have to remove the rucksac, each time the sun comes out.

The pattern shows a box-shape, made in fabric, that is sewn onto the back of the cape, the cape fabric cut away, allowing the cape to cover the rucksac. The sizes of the box are only suggestions – measure your rucksac fully laden to get the correct measurements.

NEW ZIP-CAPE

This style of cape makes use of an open-ended zip fastener down the front to allow the cape to be put on easier than before but also to allow plenty of ventilation on showery/sunny days.

A box can be sewn into the back of this cape, to cover the rucksac, as described in the normal type cape above.

A fly – internal or external – should be put down the front to keep rain from going through the zip – follow the instructions for the anorak pattern.

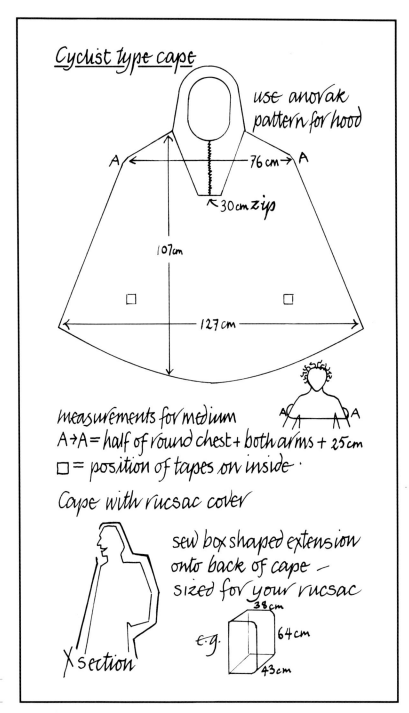

Cyclist type cape

use anorak pattern for hood

A ← 76 cm → A

← 30 cm zip

107 cm

127 cm

measurements for medium
A→A = half of round chest + both arms + 25 cm
□ = position of tapes on inside .

Cape with rucsac cover

X section

sew box shaped extension
onto back of cape —
sized for your rucsac

38 cm

e.g. 64 cm

43 cm

FIG. 30

New zips cape
with full length
open ended zips

see cyclist type cape
for measurements
+ instructions

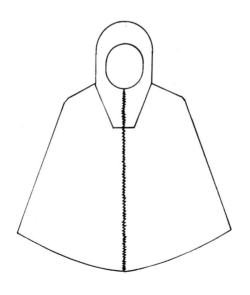

FIG. 31

Chapter 4

CUTTING OUT, MAKING-UP AND FINISHING

Before we start cutting out and making up, there are a few implements that are really essential for the successful completion of our project.

Scissors

You do really need a large pair of scissors or shears which are sharp as there is nothing worse than trying to cut these rather heavy duty fabrics with blunt scissors. You will also need a small pair of scissors for perhaps unpicking or cutting the threads when you are sewing.

Pins

You do need some pins in the making up of garments and I suggest to you that the pins with the coloured bead on the top are the best to use as they are very sharp and go through the thick proofed fabrics we are going to use.

Stapler

Although not normally found in the sewing box, you will see that a stapler becomes an essential item in our Expedition Workshop and you will also find a staple remover a useful item of equipment.

Chalk

Although normal blackboard school chalk can be used, especially if you have a sharp knife to sharpen up the end to a sort of chisel shape, the best results are obtained with real tailor's chalk which you can buy in any haberdashery shop. This enables you to draw very thin lines which means more accurate cutting out and eventually more accurate sewing.

Glue

Again glue does not usually appear in the sewing box of a conventional sewing person but you will find in our making up of these proofed items that glue is a very useful addition to our armoury. Any of the clear glues that are often used by model makers are the ones to have. We have found, as you will see, that we often glue a seam before we sew it and it is possible to sew through this clear type of glue. In the finishing it will also be useful to have rubberised type contact glue of the type used by DIY people who make wetsuits. This will be used to proof the seams when you have finished the garment but if you use this glue to start with, you find you cannot sew through it, it keeps breaking the thread.

Sewing Machines

It is not possible for me to write full instructions on how to use a sewing machine but if you have a sewing machine, or you borrow one, then read the book of instructions before you start. You should also have bits of fabric that you can practise with, that is you want bits of the proofed fabric you are going to sew and just alter the tension following the instructions in the sewing machine booklet until you have a nice seam. We are going to use the largest stitch that the machine will produce because this gives us a strong seam for our purposes.

I also suggest that you buy the largest, or rather thickest, needle that you can fit into your machine and to get these you will have to go to a good shop that specialises in sewing machines. I have found that the needles bought by people who have hobbies in leather are ideal for the purpose we are going to use them for. The leather needles have a chisel end which seem to penetrate these heavy duty fabrics for us.

I have had to cope with the machines that are available. I have never been able to ask for a specialist machine, so all the sewing I have ever done has been on ordinary domestic electric sewing machines which are quite capable of making the seams for the bulk of the work described in this book. Occasionally you will find, perhaps if you are making a rucksac and have to sew through heavy duty webbing, your sewing machine will not cope with this thickness of webbing and fabric. Then you may have to sew those on by hand, or find some person who has an industrial sewing machine to help you. However, I have never failed to get my normal domestic sewing machine to sew anything that I wanted to make. One of the tips is if you get a wax candle or, in a good haberdashery shop, a block of bees wax, rub the wax along the seam you are trying to sew and you will find that it allows the needle to penetrate really thick fabrics, acting as a lubricant for the needle.

Stitching

tension is the commonest fault in sewing
there should be equal
tension on top
and bottom threads

fabric

This is the standard stitch
of the domestic sewing machine

← top thread

top thread too tight so slacken top tension

← top thread

top thread too slack so tighten top tension

"birds nest" underneath – no tension on top
drop presser foot and rethread tension

FIG. 32

Types of seam

1 simple seam X section

sew ← glue   outside

outsides together   inside glue

2 fell or flat seam X section

sew ← glue   glue

outsides together

open up and sew down glued seam

outside view   inside view

3 french seam X section

sew   sew again

insides together   outsides together

outside view   inside view

FIG. 33

This chapter is, of course, mainly about making up the garment, but I hope also you will spend some time in the finishing off of the garment and then, although you might not think it is possible to do, some testing at home or at school by yourself. In the space available, it is just not going to be possible to give you a full detailed description of making up every item we will describe. I have, therefore, given you very full details of how to cut out and make up the anorak because during this description we will go through a lot of the details that I have developed over the years to help you make a satisfactory garment.

You will by now, I hope, have chosen a suitable fabric to make the anorak. Help in choosing a fabric is given in the table you will see in the text.

CHOICE OF FABRICS

Garment or Equipment	Type of Fabric	Comments
Waterpoof Anorak Jacket Cape Overtrousers	Heavy-duty–Long-lasting 4 + 4 Neoprene – 270 gm/sq m P.U. 135 gm/sq m	8 oz/sq yd 4 oz/sq yd
Waterpoof Anorak Jacket Cape Overtrousers	Lightweight–Less durable 2 + 2 Neoprene – 135 gm/sq m P.U. 68 gm/sq m	4 oz/sq yd 2 oz/sq yd
TENT – Outer	P.U. 68 gm/sq m Silicone elastomer 68 gm/sq m Proofed cotton 140 gm/sq m Heavy pr'd cotton 230 gm/sq m	2 oz/sq yd 2 oz/sq yd 4 oz/sq yd
TENT – Inner	Unproofed nylon Unproofed cotton	
TENT – Groundsheet	2 + 2 Neoprene 135 gm/sq m PVC 250 gm/sq m	4 oz/sq yd 8 oz/sq yd
Lining for Anorak Jacket Cape Overtrousers	Unproofed nylon Unproofed cotton Any unproofed fabric	
Gaiters	Any stiff, hard-wearing fabric 4 + 4 Neoprene 270 gm/sq m Cotton canvas 400 gm/sq m	8 oz/sq yd
Rucksacs Large	Any strong, durable fabric 4 + 4 Neoprene 270 gm/sq m Heavy P.U. 270 gm/sq m Cordura 370 gm/sq m	8 oz/sq yd 8 oz/sq yd 11 oz/sq yd
Rucksacs Small	2 + 2 Neoprene 135 gm/sq m P.U. 135 oz/sq m	4 oz/sq yd 4 oz/sq yd

▌ANORAK

At this stage, you should have a pattern cut from paper following the instructions given in Chapter 3. You should have one piece of paper which looks roughly like an anorak pressed flat which is for the main body of the anorak and you should also have a piece of paper cut out ready for the anorak hood. You will also have pieces of paper for the patterns you have cut out for the anorak pocket flaps and fly front.

You will have seen from the anorak pattern, that you know how much fabric you are going to need by deciding the length, that is C to C on the pattern, and whatever length that is, you are going to need twice that length plus 15 cm. I would also recommend that you add on 5 cm so that you have a bit of room to manoeuvre in case some of your measuring is not quite as accurate as it should be.

Before we start cutting any of these expensive fabrics, lets just remember that the success of any craft, whether it is sewing, making model aeroplanes, making a table or anything, depends on the accuracy of your marking out and then the accuracy of your cutting out. Although the accuracy required in fabric manufacture and sewing is not quite as accurate as you would have in metal work, nevertheless it must follow the pattern you have made and you must follow it accurately. You should now have a length of fabric ready to make the anorak and first of all we are going to cut off a strip across the fabric which is 150 cm wide and it is going to be a strip 15 cm wide and which we will need towards the end of the sewing to make the fly front of the garment.

You should be left with a piece of fabric which is twice the length of C to C, plus 5 cm. Fold this in half across the width so that you have a piece of fabric 150 cms wide and whatever the C to C measurement you have decided upon.

Now you see the first tip that I learnt many years ago, how terribly slippery and awkward to handle some of these modern fabrics are. When you have folded your piece of fabric, and you must fold it with the RIGHT sides together, that is the side you are going to wear on the outside, take an ordinary stapler and staple down each side of the fabric so that it holds them together.

Anorak

FIG. 34

As you will see, we are going to be cutting through two layers of fabric at the same time and if they move, the layer underneath will not be cut out accurately. Traditional sewing teaches us to use pins but I have found for some purposes like this, stapling is much more positive and a very quick system and nearly everybody has a stapler. If you are going to do a lot of this, I suggest that you go to a stationer's shop and purchase for about 40p, a staple remover, which is a little gadget that allows you to go along afterwards and remove the staples quickly and efficiently.

So you are looking at your fabric with the proofed side uppermost and the two right sides together. Down each side of the fabric where you have stapled, the fabric should look ragged or rather hairy because this is the edge of the fabric where it is woven and is called the selvedge. Take the selvedge from one side and fold it over to the selvedge at the other side and press the fabric down so that when you open it, you should see a line running down the middle of your fabric which is going to be the centre front of your anorak. With a straight edge and some chalk, draw a line down where this fold has been made on the fabric. With a straight edge you can also draw a line along the top folded edge, that is the A to A line on the garment.

Now you should have your paper pattern that you have cut out following the instructions in Chapter 3 which should have a fold down the centre. This represents the centre front of the garment and you lie this mark on the chalk mark down the centre of the fabric that you are going to cut out. The paper pattern should be just the width of the fabric although the fabric may be just a little wider, but if you line up the two centre front marks then this is the position to lie the paper pattern on the fabric.

Holding the pattern still, you are going to draw round the paper pattern. You can now remove the paper pattern because you should have drawn round this onto the fabric.

Remember there is **NO** seam allowance on the pattern.

You are therefore going to cut out 3 cm bigger than the chalk mark you have made on the fabric. This is the seam allowance.

With a good sharp pair of shears or large scissors cut out the fabric 3 cm (1 inch) bigger than the pattern marks you have drawn on the fabric. You should now have a piece of fabric which looks roughly the shape of an anorak with the sleeves held out from the sides, and you will have two pieces left which you have cut away from under the arms for you to make the hood and the pockets.

You will not have been able to leave a seam allowance on the ends of the sleeves because the fabric is not wide enough. For most people we are going to add bits on anyway so it does not matter that you have not got the necessary seam allowance there.

Anorak Hood

You should have cut out the pattern for the anorak hood according to the instructions in Chapter 3 and you will see that two of the pieces you have cut out from the main fabric will easily make the hood for you. You see instantly one advantage of having stapled together the two layers of fabric before you cut out the main anorak body, because now these two pieces you are going to use to make the anorak hood are stapled together and when you cut them out you automatically have one left side and one right side. Lie the paper anorak hood pattern on the fabric, draw round the hood pattern and remember again to cut out 3 cm bigger all round for the seam allowance.

Anorak Pockets

You will have also cut out two pieces for the anorak pockets and two pieces for the pocket flaps.

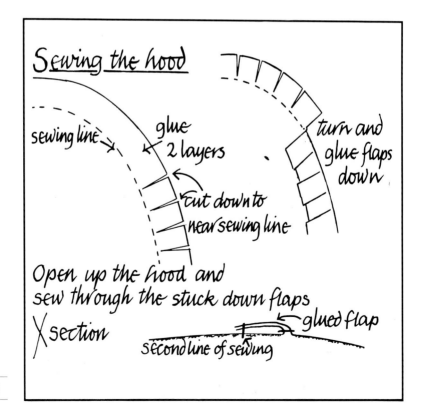

FIG. 35

MAKING UP THE ANORAK AND THE ANORAK HOOD

Ninety per cent of the difficulty in making an anorak with a hood is in getting the hood on to the main body of the anorak. This is because you are trying to sew a straight bit of fabric, that is the hood, onto a round shape, which is the neck hole, and, therefore, I suggest to everybody that while you are still fresh and keen, we get the hood on first. Once you have the hood on, the rest is all very simple because it is just flat, straight sewing.

Anorak Hood

The first seam you are going to make is to sew the two pieces of the anorak hood together. With a straight stitch you are going to sew from R to S on the anorak hood pattern, joining the two halves of the hood together. Now you are going to use the first of our tips in order to make the sewing so much easier.

Glue

Remove any pins or staples that you have had in the R to S line which you have now sewn along. Take a tube of the clear glue described above and run a little of the glue between the two layers

of fabric which will then be stuck together. Next, with a sharp pair of scissors, around the curve on the R to S seam you are going to cut down, stopping short of the sewing by about 5 mm, and snip about every 3 cm around the curve. Run the clear glue around the hood and fold over the seam allowance and stick it down and you will see why we have snipped the bits around the curved part of the hood. These will lie flat when you glue them down. This technique will be seen in more detail if you do not understand it, in Figure 35.

When you have stuck down this seam allowance, open up the two halves of the hood and sew through the stuck down seam allowance. This is illustrated in more detail under the seam notes.

The Magic Oval

Following the instructions on the anorak hood pattern, you will cut an oval from cardboard and will have drawn on it according to the instructions a cross which is 2.5 cm from the back edge and 10.5 cm from the front edge.

This oval will represent the SEWING LINE for attaching the hood to the anorak body and represents the length S to T on the anorak hood pattern, which is just a little over 28 cms.

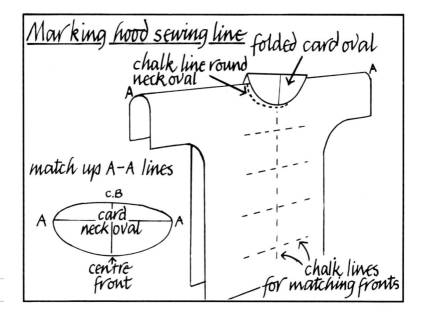

FIG. 36

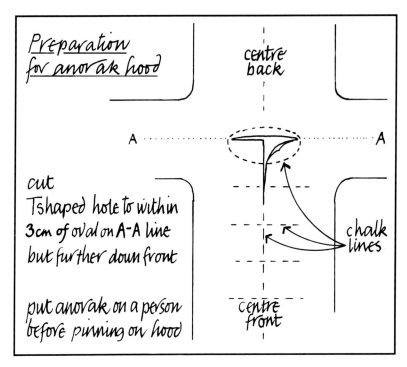

Preparation for anorak hood

centre back

A · A

cut T shaped hole to within 3 cm of oval on A-A line but further down front

chalk lines

put anorak on a person before pinning on hood

centre front

FIG. 37

MAIN BODY OF THE ANORAK

We now return to the fabric you have cut out to make the main body of the anorak. Once again, we have a technique which goes against traditional sewing teaching. I want you to take the main piece of fabric that you have cut out and turn it so that the RIGHT side of the fabric is now to the outside. In other words, you will be looking at the anorak as you are going to wear it. I want you to take the stapler and staple together the two pieces, that is the front and the back, with the fold across the A to A line. Staple together around the seam that is the underarm seam. If you staple them about one centimetre in you will not damage the fabric at all because you should have a 3 cm seam allowance. We turn the fabric the right way out and staple it in this manner, so that you can put on this garment as though it is an anorak. Lying the two pieces stapled together, you have down the centre front a chalk line and across the A to A line you should have drawn a chalk mark. Will you now draw a line about 8 cm down the centre back position. Picking up the fabric between your fingers, you should be able to separate the two layers and see that you have a cross which is the centre front, the centre back and the A to A line.

Taking the magic oval that you have cut out in cardboard, you can place the cross that you have drawn on this oval to coincide with the cross on your fabric and drawn round the oval. This represents the SEWING LINE for the hood. See figure 6.

Picking up the fabric at the centre of the cross, snip a little hole so that you can get the point of the scissors between the two layers. Cut along the A to A line for 7 cm, each side the centre front. DO NOT CUT DOWN THE CENTRE BACK LINE AT ALL but cut down the centre front line about 30 cms and you should have a t-shaped cut which is big enough to get your head through.

You are now going to find a friend who you will persuade to put on the anorak that you have stapled together, with the head through the t-shaped hole in the middle of the oval. Take the hood that you have already made up and pin it onto the main body of the anorak while the friend is wearing it. I find that this is the best way to ensure that you get the hood in the right position in all dimensions. See Figure 36.

Before you start pinning the hood on, it helps if you get the glue and turn up 3 cm on the T to S line on the anorak hood and glue this 3 cm seam allowance up inside the hood.

With someone wearing the body of the anorak, pick up the hood and put it in position. You can find the centre back of the hood and you can find the centre back on the main body of the anorak as you have already drawn a chalk mark in this position. You will now see that you have an oval shape drawn on the outside of the anorak that you can follow, pinning round the T to S line of the anorak hood. Start at the centre back and work towards the centre front, stopping the pins $1\frac{1}{2}$ cm from the centre front. Come back to the centre back and work round the other side of the oval, stopping $1\frac{1}{2}$ cm from the centre of the anorak body.

Pinning

For this anorak hood seam we have found that if you pin with the pins across the seam you are going to sew, with care, you can sew over these pins so that you do not have to take them out as you sew, which is the normal practice. This makes the task of this tricky seam much easier. See Figure 38.

When you have pinned the hood on to the main body of the anorak, the most important thing is to make sure that the two bottom edges of the anorak hood are level with each other on the main body of the anorak. I am not bothered whether you have a little tuck in the back of the hood through poor sewing, but if you have the two edges of the anorak hood at different levels, the whole garment will look home made and you will not be very happy about it. You must therefore make sure that these two bottom edges are level with each other.

When you are happy with the pinning on of the anorak hood, you can take your shears and cut down the centre FRONT of the anorak to the bottom. This enables you to take off the anorak like a jacket and it makes the sewing you are about to do much easier.

Canoeing Anorak

If you are a keen canoeist and you are going to make what is the traditional canoeing anorak where you would only have a short zip of about 30cm, of course you would not cut all the way down the centre front as we have just described, but cut down the length of the zip you are going to use.

Sewing on the Anorak Hood

This is the trickiest seam in the whole operation but if you have pinned the hood on following the oval that you have drawn on the main body of the anorak and you have put the pins up and down across the seam, you will find it possible to do with a little care. You must start at the centre back of the hood and sew round slowly to the centre front, stopping $1\frac{1}{2}$ cm from the centre front, then, going to the centre back of the hood, sew round the other side of the oval, stopping $1\frac{1}{2}$ cm from the centre front. With one row of straight stitching in, the anorak hood is quite firm but I would suggest that you then take out the pins and do another row of

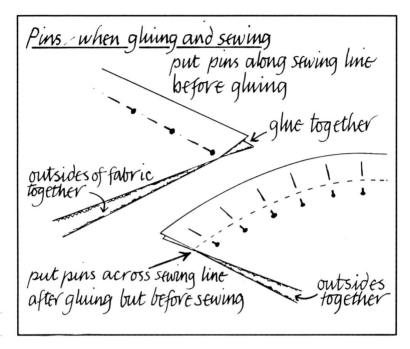

Pins - when gluing and sewing

put pins along sewing line before gluing

glue together

outsides of fabric together

put pins across sewing line after gluing but before sewing

outsides together

FIG. 38

straight stitching about 4mm from the first row. This just makes sure the hood is firmly attached to the body of the anorak.

Seam Allowance on the Oval

You will see I have not allowed you to cut an oval where you are going to sew the hood on. This is because I have found that most beginners at sewing cut the oval far too big as they forget that the seam allowance is on the INSIDE of the oval, not on the outside. So the actual size of hole that you need is very small and I have found this method of cutting a T, putting on the anorak, pinning the hood on as you go, is the safest and most efficient way of getting a hood in the right place. Of course, if you are a skilled seamstress and have had a lot of experience in sewing you can put the hood on using more traditional methods.

I now proceed with other parts of the anorak and go back to finish the inside of the hood when I come to put the lining in.

Anorak Zip Fastener

Using the gluing technique you will find that inserting a zip down the centre front of the anorak becomes childs play. First get the glue and run a little ribbon of glue down each side of the centre front and turn in $1\frac{1}{2}$ cm and glue down this seam to the inside of the anorak. You will need an open ended heavy duty zip the length of the anorak from where the hood stops to within 3 cm of the finished length of the anorak.

With care you can run a very thin ribbon of glue down one side of the fabric part of the zip. Taking the centre front of the anorak, carefully press this onto the zip starting the bottom of the hood level with the top of the slider of the zip when it is fully closed. Then go along and pin the anorak where you have glued it to the zip. Again if you put the pins across the line of the sewing you will not have to remove them when you sew.

Take the other half of the zip and pin it down the other side of the anorak and, again, this is where you must take great care to get the two halves of the zip level. That is so that when the zip is done up the anorak hood sides are level with each other. Take a bit of trouble and time to get them level if they are not level the first time you pin them.

When sewing in the zip I suggest that you start at the top and sew down to the bottom and do this on each side. One good row of stitching is quite adequate. The zip should be sewn so that it is a little way from the teeth and the slider does not catch in the fabric of the anorak.

Anorak Pockets

From the anorak pattern you will see that you should have two 25 cm squares of fabric which you have turned in 1 cm all round and glued down, sewing across one of these turned down seams which will become the top edge of the pocket and you will finish with a pocket that is 23 cm by 22 cm.

The pocket flaps are made from the two pieces of fabric 15 cm by 25 cm folded in half and sewn down each side so we have a flap 23 cm by 7 cm.

At this stage you can sew on the touch and close fastening onto the pockets and flap and I suggest that you sew on two pieces 5 cm long separating them by about 3 cm both on the pockets and the flaps.

Where on earth do you put the anorak pockets? Well again the best way is to get a friend to put on the anorak or put on the anorak yourself and say where you need the pocket. You know just where you would like it to be so that someone can mark where the top edge of the pocket is going to be. Again you must spend time and make sure that the edge of the pocket near to the zip is parallel to the zip and equally you must make sure that the two pockets are level with each other as nothing looks more amateurish than a pocket that is skew-whiff or one pocket is higher or lower than the other. When you have marked the pockets I suggest pinning them on with several pins so that they stay in place while you sew them. Start at the top edge of one pocket and sew down the side and across the bottom then sew up the second side. The pocket flaps are sewn across just outside the top edge of the pocket.

Waterproof Pocket

From the years of experience I have had in protective clothing it does not seem possible to provide a waterproof pocket on the outside of a garment, so I suggest that if you wish to carry things in the anorak pocket that have to be kept dry then you should put these items in a polythene bag and then in the pocket. Alternatively, if it is a map or some other item that you need to keep dry and it is too large for the anorak pockets, you can sew on pockets to the lining. They are inside the anorak and therefore keep dry.

Fly Front

The fly front is a means of keeping the rain from going through the zip. If you put some silicone floor polish on the zip it not only helps to lubricate the slider up and down but you will also find very little rain does enter it. Of course we also have to think of the wind.

The fly front will consist of a strip of fabric the finished length of the anorak plus 10 cm for seams which, when folded and sewn in half, produces a fly front 8 cm wide.

Internal Fly

Personally I like the fly inside the anorak which means I take an 8 cm wide strip and sew it to the side of the anorak which has the zip slider and sew it just inside the line of stitching that is holding on the zip. You will then see that if rain or wind does penetrate the zip, it is stopped by this piece of fabric inside the zip.

External Fly

If you wish you may use the more traditional method of having an external fly. You sew on the 8 cm wide strip to the outside of the anorak and you will keep the free edge of this strip in position by having a length of touch and close fastener sewn to the edge of the strip and onto the anorak body. A diagram of these two fly fronts is shown in the text in Figure 39.

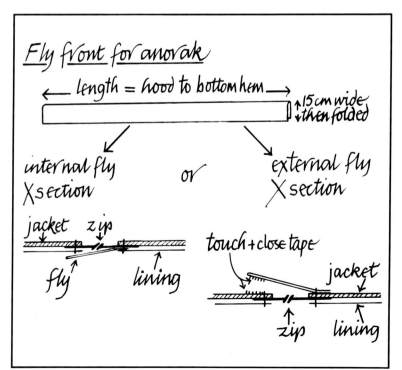

FIG. 39

Underarm Seams

The two underarm seams on the main body of the anorak should be sewn together with one good row of stitching. Glue the seams and then clip and glue the seam as for the hood. It is not possible to make a full seam under the arm but one good row of stitching, with the seam stuck down, is quite adequate.

Lining for the Anorak

The lining will be of a non-proofed fabric and almost anything will suffice. I personally use a nylon taffeta which seems to be quite adequate and is very cheap. Cut out and make up the lining exactly as you have made the outer anorak garment. So you end up with a lining that looks like an anorak onto which you have sewn the hood. Fixing the lining in the anorak is quite simple with one of our techniques using the glue. Take the main anorak body, that is the anorak made from the proofed fabric, and turn this inside out. You will see that the seam where you have sewn the hood onto the anorak may look a little ragged and so you can clip the bits off the hood and anorak so that they will lie flat around the seam and glue them which ever way they want to go, up or down it does not matter, but just make them flat ready to put in the lining. With the main body of the anorak INSIDE OUT get a friend to put on the anorak. Get the lining and have that the RIGHT way out, so you are going to put the inside of the lining onto the inside of the anorak and get the person to put on the lining over the top of the anorak that they are already wearing.

With the tube of clear glue run a generous amount around the neck seam of the hood anorak and a generous amount of glue on the centre seam that you have sewn on the hood. Picking up the lining, find the t-shaped junction where the neck seam joins the centre seam of the hood and stick this to the same point on the anorak. That has located the position of the lining. Then press the centre of the seam of the hood onto the glue that you have put on the centre seam of the anorak and similarly press the neck seam of the hood round the neck seam of the anorak towards the centre front of the anorak. This gluing has now fixed the position of the lining and the anorak to each other and this gluing is quite adequate for these two seams because we do not wish to have more sewing than is necessary.

The length of the lining sleeves is usually shorter than the length of the anorak sleeves because we have sewn on cuff like pieces to make the anorak sleeve longer. Personally I do not bother extending the lining sleeves but I merely glue them down where they finish naturally inside the anorak sleeve.

Turn in and glue $1\frac{1}{2}$ cm of the lining down the centre front, glue this seam down each side of the zip. The only sewing on the lining is a row of stitches down each side of the zip.

Turn up and sew the bottom edge of the lining, making it 3 cm shorter than the anorak. Do not fasten the lining to the bottom of the anorak – you can then go up inside between the lining and anorak to reproof the neck seams if necessary.

Finishing the Anorak

Trap the lining under the anorak fabric. The first row of sewing makes a tunnel for the draw cord. Sew strips of fabric on the bottom edge of the sleeves if necessary.

The first, and luckily the easiest, storm cuff is very weather-proof but can be "let-off" in moderate weather to give ventilation.

For canoeists and some yachtsmen a second strip of wetsuit neoprene, made into a cuff, can be kept in the pocket and rolled onto the sleeve when necessary.

Finishing the Seams

The life of the anorak will depend on the effort you take in finishing the seams.

If you are lazy and do nothing the seams will last a while. The best anoraks and jackets have taped seams, that is a strip of proofed fabric, preferably the lightweight neoprene, stuck over the seam. If possible use the glue used to make wetsuits, otherwise one of the impact adhesives will do.

If you have no fabric, paint a generous layer of clear glue over the seam.

OVERTROUSERS

I would suggest that you read the notes at the beginning of
Chapter 4 which give a few hints on handling the fabrics, cutting
out and so on. Making overtrousers is one of the easiest tasks in
this chapter, but still you can save many pounds by making
yourself a really super pair of waterproof overtrousers, even if
you have no previous experience of sewing. The reason that overtrousers are so simple is that they do not usually have a fly and
80% of the difficulties in making an ordinary pair of trousers or
jeans is getting the fly neat and tidy and flat. Figure 12 illustrates
a point that you must bear in mind when making overtrousers
without a fly and it shows that you cannot put on a normal pair
of trousers unless you have opened the fly, So, with overtrousers,
they always look rather big around the waist as the waist has to
be big enough to pass over your hips.

You should have four pieces of paper cut from Figure 4 which
will represent Right Back, Right Front, Left Back, Left Front of
your trousers. You should have cut a piece of fabric 152 cm wide
which will be used to make the overtrousers and the length of
fabric you require is the outside leg measurement plus a few cms
(say 7 cm) to allow for seams and the turnover for the tunnel
round the top of the trousers.

It is well worth cutting the four pieces of pattern to make the
trousers because when you lie them on the fabric you can move
them around and get the best use of the fabric. You will have to
be very fat before you cannot position the four pieces of the fabric
across the 152 cm width. Remember you must leave 6 cm between
each piece of fabric so that when you cut out the shapes you can
leave the 3 cm seam allowance that we suggest is suitable when
you are making a waterproof garment.

It is well worth fitting a zip of about 30 cm or 40 cm to the bottom
of the outside seam of each leg, as this means you can have a
tapered leg and for walkers it means that you can take the overtrousers on and off without removing your boots. This is a boon
when you are out on a dirty or muddy hillside.

The first job for you to do is to find the Left Front and the Right Front and you are going to join these two pieces together sewing the seam that runs down the front where the fly would normally be, to the crutch underneath. Take the two pieces of fabric with the right sides together and pin them with the two curves matching each other. You should have a chalk mark showing you where to sew, that is 3 cm in from the edge of the fabric, leaving the 3 cms seam allowance. Using a straight stitch, which should be the largest stitch on your sewing machine, sew these two pieces together, starting at the waist and going carefully round the curve to the edge of the fabric which is going to be underneath your crutch.

Find the two Back pieces, that is Right Back and Left Back, pin them together in the same way and sew the seam which is from the waist round underneath your bottom to your crutch.

These two seams are the seams that tear (if any seam tears on overtrousers) because this is where all the tension is put when you wear trousers. Therefore we are going to strengthen up these two seams so that, hopefully, they will not tear during their life.

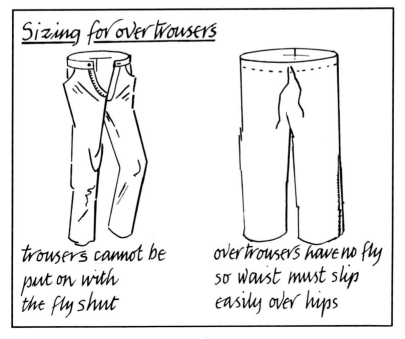

Sizing for over trousers

trousers cannot be put on with the fly shut

over trousers have no fly so waist must slip easily over hips

FIG. 40

Taking the two front pieces that you should have sewn together with one row of strong straight stitching from the waist round the curve to the crutch, you are going to use the technique that is shown in Figure 35 that we use to strengthen the seam on the hood. With a tube of glue open the two layers of fabric and run a thin line of glue between the two layers and stick them together. Then with a sharp pair of small scissors, clip the seams which you have just stuck together every 3 cm or so, stopping before you reach the sewing line on the bit of the seam that is curved, you do not need to clip where the seam is straight. Taking the tube of glue run a generous amount of glue on the fabric inside the sewing line about 3 cm wide and take the two layers of fabric that you have glued together and bend them over and stick them down wherever you put the glue. You will see now why you have to clip on the curves and you should end up with the whole seam stuck together, turned over and glued down. Now you must open the two pieces of fabric so that you can sew through the seam that you have stuck down. And if you have zig-zag on your machine, I suggest that you zig-zag down this seam as this makes a very strong stitch which will not break or crack easily when you stretch the seam. If you do not have zig-zag just sew one good row of straight sewing down this seam.

Repeat this process with the two back pieces so that we end up with the Left Front and the Right Front sewn together and the Left Back and the Right Back sewn together.

You are now going to sew together the two back pieces to the two front pieces and if you open up the two pieces of fabric you have sewn together and lie them on top of each other with the right sides together, lining up the two seams that you have just sewn. That is the Centre Front seam and the Centre Back seam. You are going to sew the seam that runs from your left ankle up the inside of your left leg, under your crutch and down the inside seam to the right ankle. Pin this seam and run a little bit of glue between the two layers of fabric to hold them together while you sew with the same straight stitch as large as you can make it. We are now going to strengthen up this seam just as you did with the first seams, gluing the two layers together and then turning the

seam over and sticking it down, clipping the seam as you did before where it is in the curve. Sew round, as you did before, with a zig-zag stitch or a straight stitch as you wish. We are now going to do the outside leg seam but, if you are going to put zips in the bottom of the trousers, you should put in the zips before you complete this outside leg seam.

If you are going to put in zips, read the technique for putting in the anorak zip and follow those general ideas. A zip about 30 cm long is the usual length to put in. A medium weight spiral zip or a medium weight tooth zip is suggested. When you have sewn in the zips, complete the seam up to the waist line and you can now see for the first time the shape and size of your trousers. I think if you look on the outside sewing of the trousers you will see that the top end of the zip represents a place where you might easily tear the seam of fabric when you are putting these trousers on or off in a hurry in the pouring rain on a mountain. Therefore I suggest that you get a piece of fabric about 6 cm square, turn in 1 cm and stick it down all round and sew this strengthening piece of fabric over the top end of the zip and onto the fabric of the trousers.

You can now turn the trousers with the right sides out and put them on to try them for size. This is also the time for you to find the natural waist line and turn over the trousers and mark, or pin, this position which gives you the upper edge of the trousers. You will need a friend to turn up the bottom end of the trousers to the length that you require.

Take the trousers off. Turn them inside out and we are ready to complete the waistband. You should find a piece of fabric about 10cm long and about 7cm wide. Find the Centre Front seam and stick this piece of fabric inside the trousers covering the Centre Front seam and going across the line you have marked for the top edge of your trousers. This is a piece of strengthening material because now you should put in two medium sized eyelets about 3cm each side of the Centre Front seam and about 1cm down from the finished top edge of the trousers. The eyelets are for you to bring out the draw cord when you have finished the overtrousers.

With the eyelets in, all you have to do is turn over the waist line where you have marked it and sew round about 3cm down from the finished top edge to make a tunnel for the draw cord. I much prefer a draw cord to elastic because you can change the tension of a draw cord and if you are a bit hot and sticky you can let it off but with elastic you are stuck with this tight band round your waist. The bottom of the trousers you have marked and these can be turned up and sewn round quite easily. The side leg seams, the seam round the waist band and the bottom of the trousers, I suggest do need sticking down and some proofing. This can consist of putting a layer of the clear plastic glue or if you are really going to make super trousers, taking strips of the fabric or some similar lightweight proof material and sticking a strip over each seam with glue.

Salopettes or High Sailing Trousers

The patterns for these two items are really the overtrouser pattern with a piece sewn onto the waist bringing them up to just under each arm and covering the chest and back. They are made up in exactly the same way, starting with the two centre seams, that is sewing together the Left Front and the Right Front, the Right Back and the Left Back. It is possible just to have a draw cord under the arms but many people do prefer to have a short zip running down the chest, but not going down into the crutch area where a fly would normally go. I think both salopettes and high sailing trousers do need a bracer strap over each shoulder and this should be made of elastic because if you watch when you bend, you increase the length of the back quite a lot, several inches in fact, and you must have an elastic bracer.

Overtrousers, Double Seat

If you are a sailor then you are often sitting on a wet plank on board ship and often scuffing about on a boat deck so that a double seat is pretty essential for you. Also patches over the knees are not a bad idea either.

I have found the best and easiest way of double seating over-trousers is to make up to the pattern that you have used what is, in effect, a pair of shorts, with these made up I just drop them inside the overtrousers with the two proof layers together and stick them in around the bottom of the trouser legs and round the waist. Then a row of sewing round the waist secures them for ever and you have no stitching around the double seat to let water in.

Even if you are not a sailor scuffing about on wet decks but a walker, I would suggest a similar pair of shorts made in non-proof lining material put inside your overtrousers in the way that the double seat is put in would make the wearing of the overtrousers much better. I do not know anywhere that you can buy lined overtrousers so you are going to give yourself a unique garment.

■ OVERTROUSERS: SPECIAL DISABLED ETC

I developed the pattern for these overtrousers at the request of many disabled people that I met at outdoor centres, who complained it was not possible to buy decent waterproof trousers for people who are often paralysed from the waist downwards and find it difficult to put on normal trousers. They are merely a pair of overtrousers with an open ended zip down the front crease of each trouser leg which enables the zip to be unzipped and opened so that you now have a flat garment. A paraplegic can put this garment on the bed, get themselves on top of it zip up and hey presto they have on a pair of overtrousers.

Two points to note with the overtrousers are that the legs do want to be very wide because often they will have to cover a calliper and in any event someone who is paralysed from the waist finds it very difficult to put on tight fitting trousers because they cannot push the legs into the trouser legs if they are tight. Also people who are paralysed can do immense damage with a days sailing or canoeing to find they have a horrible sore where something in the boat has been rubbing and because of the paralysis, they did not feel this damage taking place. Therefore I cut out the shape of the outer overtrousers in fibre pile fabric, so that when zipped up the trousers are lined with warm and cushioning fabric. The fibre pile lining was held in with pieces of touch and close tape so that if anyone was incontinent, it could be removed and washed in the washing machine quite easily.

FIBRE-PILE FABRICS

You should practise sewing fibre pile fabrics before you start sewing up your garments as they are rather unusual fabrics in two respects. First, of course, they are very thick fabrics, that is why I suggest that you cut seams 6 cm wide if there is enough fabric. Otherwise, when you sew, the foot of the sewing machine keeps running off the fabric. Then we are really using these fabrics the wrong way out so we are going to have the smooth side of the fabric outwards and the fur side inwards, which means you are going to be sewing with the pile sides facing outwards and this makes things a bit more difficult. If you practise a little on some strips of fabric you will find that it is possible to sew these fabrics and make respectable garments with a little effort.

FIBRE-PILE JACKET OR PULLOVER

This is the simplest pattern for making a jacket or pullover as it is cut in one main piece very much like the anorak pattern, so you are only going to have two main seams to sew, that is the two underarm seams and, of course, the neck and hood.

If you follow the instructions for fitting the hood to the anorak you will find that you can sew on the hood to this fibre pile jacket quite easily. However, many people prefer to have just a stand-up collar on such a jacket and you follow the same general instructions, but just putting on the stand-up collar which will end up about 5 cm tall.

Putting a zip down the front of the fibre pile jacket can represent problems but I have found that the best way to do this is to fold in about 2 cm of fabric all down the front and pin it firmly. I then sew this 2 cm seam in with one good row of stitching which keeps it flat while you pin in the zip and you can then sew the zip in quite easily.

Many people prefer to have an elastic cuff round the bottom of the sleeves and round the bottom of the jacket. These elastic webbings can be bought in many colours from a good haberdasher. The difficulty in sewing them is that you have to stretch them around the seam while you sew them, so that when you have finished the elastic can pull back and you have the effect on the waist and the sleeves.

Figure 8 shows three styles of pocket that you may want to choose from. The first pattern shows you the more traditional pocket put on to these jackets which I personally do not like because items put into these pockets tend to fall out rather easily, I prefer the second type of pocket which has a square pocket and a flap held down with touch and close fastening. The third style on Figure 8 shows what many manufacturers are now doing, putting a pocket which is a hand-warmer style and you may choose this at your will.

■ FIBRE PILE JACKET WITH INSET SLEEVES

Figure 7 shows the more traditional style of fibre pile jacket which will have an inset sleeve. The measurements are listed for a medium sized jacket with suggestions of how to make it bigger or smaller, but it would be as well, if you are not skilled at sewing, to try and get some old fabric to make a pattern before you cut out your precious fibre pile material. When you have cut out the

pattern leaving very wide seams as suggested with all fibre pile materials, I think you should tack the whole thing together just to try on the garment to make sure it is about the right size, the only difficult part of this pattern is setting in the sleeve.

When you have cut out the parts of the jacket you should tack together first the main body, that is tack together the shoulder seams which will give you the main body of the garment that you can now slip on and try for size. Take the sleeve pieces and tack them together along the line marked 'L' on the pattern so that you have a right and left sleeve. With the sleeve the right way out and the body of the garment the wrong way out, you can slip the sleeve into the arm hole and tack round the arm hole to try the sleeve. When you are satisfied with the fit, the first seam is to sew round the two arm holes to secure the sleeves in the main body of the garment. The hood and collar can be put on following the general instructions in the anorak pattern.

Elasticated webbing is often put round the bottom of the sleeves and round the bottom of the garment but these are not necessary and are a matter of choice. Figure 8 shows three styles of pocket that you may wish to sew onto your jacket.

FIBRE-PILE TROUSERS/ SALOPETTES

These are quite simply made following the pattern given for the waterproof trousers/salopettes. They are often used as a warm lining to these waterproof garments or may be covered with a non-proofed nylon fabric to make them more wind-proof when out skiing or walking in the winter.

SEAMS IN FIBRE-PILE MATERIALS

You will have made one row of straight stitching to sew whatever seam you are doing and you will be left with the wide seams that I have recommended to you. To finish off these seams I find, unless you have access to an overlocker, the easiest way to deal with them is to cut one side of the seam back to about 6 mm and cut the other side of the seam back to about 12 mm which overlaps the shorter one. I then just sew down with a row of stitching along the longer side and this gives quite a reasonable finish which, after all, is inside the garment.

SHELTER

I think it would be possible to fill a whole book just dealing with the design and making of tents because there seem to be endless varieties and shapes that one could make.

I have included fairly detailed patterns of several standard tents which are quite sufficient for you to make. Perhaps if you make one of the simpler ones you will get the bug and go on to design and make a tent to suit your particular need. Walk round one of the many camping exhibitions often associated with garden centres where you will be able to see an endless variety of tents from which you may get inspiration.

◼ GENERAL HINTS ON MAKING A TENT

This list is just a few general ideas that apply to the making of any tent or any large item that you are going to use.

It is well worthwhile, before you start making a tent, to make a model in thin cardboard so that you get the general idea and can then usually see the best way of putting things together.

Having made the model you can then just sit and work out the best way of using the fabric to get the most efficient use out of the width and, in this way, you will find you save many metres of material.

In all crafts, which includes sewing, but especially in making tents where you are going to be sewing seams sometimes 2 or 3 metres long, the accurate marking out and cutting out of the parts is vital, otherwise you will find the tent lopsided or some other fault.

With a long seam the system which I have used over many years, of pinning a seam and then gluing the two parts of the seam together, really pays off. The glue is, as always, Clear Bostik No 1 or similar clear glue and a small amount between the two sides of the seam after you have pinned it will just glue them together and they will not move at all while you are sewing them. You must use this type of glue and not the rubbery type of glues because it is not possible to sew through the rubbery types. You can, however, use these afterwards to help proof the seams or stick tape on to the seams.

All seams should be felled seams wherever possible as tents do really take a battering when they are put in high winds.

All the seams, wherever possible, should have some thin tape sewn into them or even some very thin nylon cord. If you are doing a fell seam it is possible, when you are turning over, to produce the fell by glueing the tape inside the fell before you finally sew it and, again, the glueing just makes this an easy operation. If you have a zig-zag motion on the sewing machine, zig-zagging down the fell with the tape inside it produces a very strong seam.

Special care must be taken with any seam where it is under tension (like the seam down the ridge of a tent) and it is well worthwhile just taking extra care with this type of seam and making sure that you have a very strong piece of sewing.

All seams should be sealed in some way because, with the strain of being battered by the winds, all seams tend to be pulled open and will then leak. Sealing seams can be done in a variety of ways, just putting on some glue could be sufficient, but the best tents would have a taped seam, that is a piece of thin proofed fabric stuck on the inside with a good adhesive.

We are using rather thin fabrics for the groundsheets in order to keep down the total weight of the tent and, with care, these will last several years. If, however, you find that, when you kneel on wet grass, water does come through, then if you take ordinary silicone floor polish and spread this on the outside of the ground-sheet it will restore the waterproof quality of the fabric.

Wherever on the tent you put a loop of tape to hold a guy rope or loops round the groundsheet for pegging down the groundsheet, or you put a D ring, then a square of about 6 cm around these points is necessary just to strengthen up that area of the fabric.

Zips cannot be heavy duty because quite often you are going round curves so, therefore, a medium weight tooth zip or a heavy duty spiral zip should be used.

Finally, do make decent stuff bags in which to put the tent, the inner tent and poles. So often I see in shops quite an expensive tent which has such a poor stuff bag or the bag is so small that it is impossible to get the poles or the tent in easily. A pattern for stuff bags is given at the end of the section on rucksacs.

◼ BIVI BAG

Figure 10 shows the simplest of all shelter items, a simple bivi bag, a piece of fabric of about 2 metres, or longer if you wish, folded over and sewn across the bottom down one side. A tunnel at the top for the draw string completes this very useful item. If you take real trouble to fold it and get all the air out you will find it will go in to a package of about 10cm by 8cm by 3cm and in this form is very usefully carried with you in your pocket.

Double Bivi Bag

By using two lengths of fabric and sewing them together down each side and across the bottom you make a bivi bag that is now 150cm wide and 230cm long. This is very useful if you have an emergency and need to take someone in the bivi bag with you.

Leaders Bivi Bag

Figure 10 is just an extension of the double bivi bag making a rather larger sack, with the idea that a leader could use it in an emergency to give shelter to several people. It is just sewn together with decent seams and tags on so that, in fact, it does become a tent when tied up to a tree or rocks or even with using rucksacs to hold it up.

 # HOOPED BIVI TENT

This very effective but lightweight 1/2 person bivi tent is the next step along our road to a circus marquee. It is an extension of a large bivi bag into which we are going to make tunnels to insert very small fibre glass rods like thick knitting needles, which when inserted produce 3 hoops and so the fabric is held off your body and you will find it is much more comfortable in this way. This tent, complete with fibre glass rods, guy ropes, tent pegs and everything else, will weigh only about 500gms and can be packed down into a very small bag.

From Figure 11 you will see you need to sew together the floor and the lightweight fabric which will be the top of the tent so that you end up with a piece which is 272cm long, (that is 190cm plus 41cm plus 41cm) and 203 wide, (that is 127cm plus 76cm). You are going to mark out accurately and sew on 6 pieces of the 3cm nylon tape and these are sewn on with a row of stitching down each side making a tunnel for the poles. The 6 pieces are sewn on in the position shown on the pattern. There are also 2 pieces of tape sewn on like this which are along the ridge of the tent. You will see by using this method that nearly all the sewing is done with this large piece of fabric flat and you are not trying to sew into a three dimensional tent. Make a tunnel at each end for a draw cord, sew on the loops as shown on the pattern and the last seam you are going make is to bring the left-hand edge of the fabric over and sew it on to the right-hand edge of the floor, thus making the tunnel. But you only have this one seam to do which is a bit tricky because you are having to sew with this tube shaped object. The 6 tunnels to contain the fibre glass rods are not open where they meet the ground but the tape is turned back to make a little pocket in which sits the end of the fibre glass rod. The tent is erected by pegging out the floor and pushing the rods down into the tunnel. The shape of the tent is made by taking hold of the two ends of the fibre glass rods which are now sticking out of the tunnels near the ridge. With a small length of brass tube slipped on to one side of the fibre glass rod, you press down on the fibre glass rod and slip the other end of the rod into the tube and this jams in and makes the loop. You will have three of these to make the shape of the tent and fibre glass rods down the ridge just to give it a bit of stability. The brass tube can be bought in short lengths from any good model shop. You may find the fibre glass rods in some camping shops or even in fishing shops, where you may buy reject fishing blanks and the rods need to be 2 or 3 millimetres in diameter. In the appendix there is an address for a supplier of fibre glass rods which are purpose made for tents.

HOOPED ONE/TWO-PERSON BIVI TENT

Cutting List

No Seam Allowance

Allow 3cm for Each Seam

Main Tent
68gm P.U. or silicone elastomer

272 cm × 150 cm	1 off	Top of tent
272 cm × 75 cm	1 off	Groundsheet

Sundries

3 cm wide nylon tape	6 × 64 cm	Tunnels for rods
3 cm wide nylon tape	3 × 191 cm	Reinforcement for seams
3 cm wide nylon tape	3 × 76 cm	Ditto
3 cm wide nylon tape	8 × 8 cm	Loops for tent pegs
3 mm fibre glass rods	6 × 64 cm	For hoops
3 mm fibre glass rods	3 × 64 cm	Along ridge
Nylon cord	2 × 229 cm	Draw cords
Nylon cord	2 × 152 cm	Guy ropes
Tent pegs	About 6	

■ TWIN HEIGHT, TWO-PERSON BIVI TENT

This twin height, two-person bivi tent is one of the easiest to make, but also one of the most useful as it is very weather-proof in the low profile and you can still sit up in it when you have it in the high profile. Also the poles are going to be very easy to find because you could use almost anything from some aluminium tubing or wood or even canes.

The making up is very simple. By keeping the 5.3 metres of the main body fabric intact, I then attach the wings at each side along the edge of the roof. Do not forget to use the gluing technique mentioned in the opening paragraph of this section, where you are going to be sewing quite long seams which if you pin them and then stick the two pieces together, you will find sewing is a simple operation.

The seam where the wings join the roof of the tent definitely need taping because they will take all the strain of the winds. However, I tape as many seams as possible and down the sides and along the edges of the wings I sew some nylon tape, merely because it makes the tent last much longer.

TWIN HEIGHT, TWO-PERSON BIVI TENT

Cutting List

No Seam Allowance

Allow 3 cm for each seam

Main body of Tent
150 cm × 5.33 metres   1 off

68 gm P.U. or Silicone Elastomer

Wings

218 cm × 94 cm   1 off

68 gm P.U. or Silicone Elastomer
Cut across diagonally for wings

Walls
213 cm × 76 cm   1 off

Unproofed Nylon
Cut diagonally

Poles
51 cm with spike extra   1 off
122 cm with a hole at each end

Cross Pole folding in half

Sundries
Eyelets medium   3 off
5 cm Squares leather or fabric
3 cm wide tape   5.5 metres
Nylon cord   9 metres
Tent pegs   6 off

Reinforce eyelets
Reinforce seams
Guy ropes

SQUARE FRONT BIVI TENT (POLYTHENE)

I have included here the cutting list for a square front, 2-man bivi tent which is very similar to the twin height bivi tent but is made in heavy duty polythene. It is merely 500 gauge polythene sheet which can be bought at most garden centres and it is held together by 8 cm pressure tape which is commonly sold for sticking together packing cases etc. Although not anywhere near as robust as a fabric tent, it means that you can make a tent even if you have no access to a sewing machine and is great fun to make and can be used on simple journeys but not, of course, out in the wilds.

SQUARE FRONT BIVI TENT (POLYTHENE)

Cutting List

No Seam Allowance

Allow Generous Seams 5 cm

Tent and Floor
500 gauge polythene   2 metres wide   5.5 metres

Poles
51 cm spike extra   Wood or aluminium

Sundries
8 cm wide Pressure Adhesive Tape   1 Roll
Eyelets medium size   2 off
10 cm squares leather or fabric   Reinforce eyelets
10 cm circle rigid plastic   Stand for poles
25 cm square   3 off Unproofed fabric   Ventilation on walls
Tent pegs   4 off

HOOPED TWO-PERSON TENT

This design of tent was one of the first that I was involved with designing and helping people to make. The first one was made by two young men who had just finished an apprenticeship and were hitch-hiking round America. They made a tent to this design in thin Ventile and carried it all round America where it gave very satisfactory use and they rarely used guy-ropes because they were mostly sleeping in lay-bys and fields and found, when the ground sheet was pegged down and they were asleep in the tent, it did not move at all, it just sat there and their weight held it even in quite strong winds.

You will see that the tunnel part is made from a piece of fabric 229cm long and 279cm wide. Onto this you are going to mark accurately and sew 6 pieces of nylon tape sewn down each side so that you have made 6 tunnels in which you will insert the fibre glass rods to make the shape of the tent. There will be two pieces of tape sewn in this manner along the ridge of the tunnel.

I start cutting two lengths of fabric for the 229cm the width of the fabric, that gives me 229cm by 305cm but I make a big effort in the seam joining these two pieces of fabric because this will become the ridge of the tent, but when I have finished with the fell seam with tape inside, it is a very strong seam.

As always I sew tape along every seam where it is possible and again you will see that most of this sewing is done with the fabric flat and the last operations are to join the edge of the tent to the wall of the floor and only when you are doing the last of these seams are you dealing with a three dimensional object.

If you use open-ended zips on the porch, you will find you can sew one side of the zip to the tent and the other side to the porch and then join them by making the zip. I always sew a fly of fabric over the zips to stop the rain going through. The front and rear walls of the floor should not be fastened or sewn up because when you are going in and out of the tent you want these two walls to lie flat on the floor so that you are not tending to tear any seam.

■ HOOPED TWO-PERSON BIVI TENT

Cutting List

No Seam Allowance

Allow 3cm for each seam

Main Tent		68 gms P.U. nylon or silicone elastomer
260 × 150 cm	2 off	Join with seam at ridge
130 × 86 cm × 117 cm	4 off	Bell ends
122 × 99 cm	2 off	Doors to tent
Ground Sheet		2 + 2 Neoprene
259 × 152 cm	1 off	Includes 115 cm wall
Poles		
5 mm diam × 130 cm	6 off	Rods for hoops
5 mm diam × 57 cm	4 off	Rods for ridge
Sundries		
3 cm wide nylon tape × 130 cm	6 off	Tunnels for rods
3 cm wide nylon tape × 114 cm	2 off	Tunnels for rods on ridge
3 cm wide nylon tape × 500 cm		Reinforce seams
3 cm wide nylon tape × 80 cm		Loops for pegs
3 cm wide nylon tape × 32 cm		Loops for guys
Nylon cord		Guy ropes
Tent pegs	8 off	

BASIC RIDGE TENT

This is a basic ridge tent that has been used in some form or other for very many years and is still a good work horse providing very good adequate shelter in extremes of weather.

I usually make up the inner tent first, although I do not have any very set ideas on what order to make things. The seams on the inner tent are not quite so critical as those on the outer because they are not in the full flow of the weather, but obviously the seams on the groundsheets want to be thoroughly proofed and strong.

The making up of the fly sheet is quite simple because it is all straight forward sewing. All the seams should be felled with tape inside them and especially the seam along the ridge, where all the tension will be put and which will take all the battering of the weather. In sewing all of these seams, use the techniques listed at the beginning of this section, pinning and then gluing the seam together before you sew it, then when you are making the fold for the felling and putting the nylon tape inside the fell, the glue again just holds it all together and you will find no trouble in sewing them.

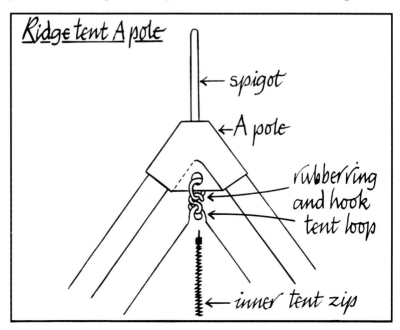

FIG. 41

 BASIC RIDGE

Cutting List

No Seam Allowance

Allow 3cm for each seam

Inner Tent

		Unproofed nylon or cotton
183 × 192 × 112 cm	2 off	Sides right and left
112 × 61 cm	3 off	Rear bell end
112 × 93 × 64 cm	2 off	Front doors (can be proofed fabric)
91 cm zip fastener	1 off	Closed end front doors
64 cm zip fastener	2 off	Closed end front doors

Ground Sheet

		2 + 2 neoprene nylon
249 cm × 127 cm	1 off	Reinforced P.V.C. an alternative

Outer Tent

		68 gm P.U. nylon or silicone elastomer
198 cm × 140 cm	2 off	Outer sides right and left
140 cm × 76 cm	6 off	Bell ends front and rear

Poles

A pole each leg 140 cm	2 off	Spike extra
203 cm hole each end	1 off	Ridge pole

Sundries

3 cm wide nylon tape	5 mtrs	Reinforce seams
3 cm wide nylon webbing	2 mtrs	Loops for tent pegs
Eyelets medium	2 off	Holes in ridge for peg spikes
4 cm squares leather or fabric	2 off	Reinforce eyelets
60 cm squares nylon net	2 off	Ventilation in doors
Tent pegs	25 off	

TRANS-RIDGE TENT

This is exactly like the previous pattern, that is, it is a ridge tent, but suddenly we have had tents appearing where the ridge is the other way. In other words, traditionally you slept along in line with the ridge, now the ridge is at 90 degrees to your body. I do not see any advantage in a trans-ridge tent, but I must confess I have no experience of using one of these tents. Making up is very straight forward, identical to making the traditional ridge tent using all the techniques mentioned there of gluing and felling seams with tape inside and then sealing all seams before use.

TRANS RIDGE TENT

Cutting List

No Seam Allowance

Allow 3 cm for each seam

Inner Tent		Unproofed nylon or cotton
142 cm × 132 cm	2 off	Slopes from ridge
142 cm × 109 cm × 91 cm	4 off	Two end triangles
91 cm zips	2 off	Closed end vertical on doors
109 cm zips	4 off	Closed ends horizontal
Ground Sheet		2 + 2 Neoprene or similar
234 cm × 152 cm	1 off	Includes 10 cm walls
Outer Flysheet		68 gm P.U. or silicone elastomer
198 cm × 132 cm	2 off	Slopes from ridge
198 cm × 142 cm × 91 cm	4 off	Triangles for bell ends
142 cm × 142 cm × 91 cm		Triangles for bell ends

Poles

102 cm spike extra	2 off	Straight poles
Or A poles 1152 cm each leg	2 off	Alternative
132 cm with hole each end	1 off	ridge pole

Sundries

3 cm wide nylon tape	10 metres	Reinforce seams
3 cm wide nylon webbing	2–3 metres	Loops tent pegs etc
Eyelets medium	2 off	Holes in ridge for spikes
Nylon cord	4–5 metres	Guy ropes
Tent pegs	About 20	

SLEEPING BAGS

I think making a good warm sleeping bag is one of the most rewarding sewing exercises that I became involved with.

I have made sleeping bags that have had a variety of fillings from standard terylene to goose down but nowadays 90% of all sleeping bags that I have made during my workshop courses are made from fibre pile fabrics, because we find they can be handled by people who have never done any sewing before and they produce a very robust, easily washable and very warm sleeping bag.

If you are experienced at sewing it is possible to make sleeping bags with down fillings. The easy way out is to purchase from the address in the appendix where the small one man business in Sheffield will sell to you the empty cover of a down sleeping bag. This is certainly worthwhile doing if you have an old bag full of down which is now leaking down because the fabric has become rather worn or perhaps torn. Perhaps also you have been to a jumble sale and been lucky enough to buy an Eider down for a pound or two. If you are going to attempt to make a sleeping bag with down filling, you must know there is a technique we developed to get the down from one bag to another or from a bag of new down into the sleeping bag, because if you try it without a bit of experience and you do it indoors, you will have down flying about the house for months afterwards. The secret is to go to a shop that sells plastic or perhaps even a garden centre and purchase a roll of thin polythene lay flat tubing about 30cm wide. You go into the garage and very gently take handfuls of the down from the old sleeping bag or from the bag of new down and you push it into the lay flat polythene tubing so that you end up with a sausage about 10 metres long full of down. Count how many tunnels you have in the new sleeping bag that you are going to fill, which will probably be about 8 or 10. Taking the sausage full of down, you cut it into the number of tunnels you require, sealing each end with some sort of paper clip so that the down is trapped in the polythene tube. You insert the tube into the fabric tunnel on the new sleeping bag cover and slowly pushing from one end you will be able to push the down into the sleeping bag, slowly withdrawing the polythene as you go. In this way you will be able to transfer most of the down from the old bag to the new bag.

■ RECTANGULAR SLEEPING BAG

This design is the traditional square, or rather rectangular, bag sold by many of the high street stores and used by thousands of people in caravans and even at home. Nothing wrong with being square, except that it occupies more space in a rucksac and is not as warm under extreme conditions as a tapered bag. However, it does have two advantages. One you can, provided the zips match, zip together two of these bags to produce a double sleeping bag which from experience I have found rather disappointing because they are rather cold, with a tunnel of cold air going between the two occupants. Second, it is convenient when unzipped because it will provide a good warm cover for the spare bed and I know many people who use these rectangular sleeping bags in that manner.

■ MUMMY-TYPE SLEEPING BAG

This is the type of sleeping bag I prefer, finding it very warm and having the advantage of being able to unzip it if I am too warm. which is not very often and be made much warmer by pulling the draw cord round ones face if you are feeling a bit chilly in the night.

The make up is fairly obvious and the seams on the fibre pile fabric do not have to be particularly tidy. I often, when joining them just overlap 5 or 6 cm and sew the two fabrics together, because you are going to cover it with some unproofed nylon. I make up the inner sleeping bag and then make up the nylon covering bag separately and just merely insert one inside the other and the two are held together only at the top edge and where the zip is sewn down the side of the bag.

■ TAPERED SLEEPING BAG WITH HOOD OR COLLAR

This is a tapered design which differs from the mummy type of bag in having a hood to cover the head, rather than pulling the mummy design around the face. Some people prefer not to have a hood but merely put a collar on to seal round the neck. This design of bag must have a zip in otherwise you would not be able to get into the bag. How long the zip is depends on personal preference, but it needs to be at least 50 or 60 cms in order to make getting into the bag a reasonable operation. I make up the fibre pile bag first then make up the nylon fabric bag and merely put one inside the other and only sew them together where the zips join and round the collar. You will find this is all the sewing that is needed.

■ RUCKSACS

I am just going to list a few general ideas when making rucksacs and not give detailed notes on each sac, because from the design it is fairly obvious how to make up these items.

General ideas when making rucksacs:

You are going to impose great strain, through the weight you are carrying in a rucksac, on the shoulder straps where they join the top of the back and where they join the base, so that the sewing at these points must be especially carefully carried out. You need the thickest needle you can buy from a good sewing machine shop in order to sew these rather heavy fabrics and certainly you are going to have to sew through the nylon webbing of the straps. If you are in difficulty in sewing any of these seams on rucksacs, you will find if you buy a piece of bees wax and rub this along the seams you are going to sew before you sew them, the wax helps you to penetrate the fabrics much easier. If you have no bees wax and cannot get it, an ordinary candle will do the job nearly as well. You want the thickest sewing thread that your machine will take, which is usually governed by the size of the eye in the needle and if you ask in a good sewing machine shop I am sure they would give you the right advice.

To make sure that the shoulder straps are very firmly attached, I buy metal rivets and just put two little rivets through each strap where they are attached to the top of the back.

The seams joining the back to the front pieces are also going to take the weight of the rucksac and need to be sewn carefully with heavy duty needles as far as possible.

Even if you buy the most expensive rucksac you may find eventually that, because of the weight, you are carrying the seams open and the contents will get wet, therefore I always have everything packed in poly bags and then have a dustbin liner inside the sac as well.

 LARGE DAY SAC

Cutting List

No Seam Allowance

Allow 3 cm for each seam

Main Body		270 gms proofed nylon
150 gms × 1.6 metres	1 off	Use cordura if available
3 cm wide × 4 metres		Nylon webbing-medium thickness
3 cm wide × 2 metres		Nylon webbing — heavy duty
3 cm wide × 2.5 metres		Nylon tape — binding pockets
Sundries		
3 cm buckles	2 off	Heavy duty-carrying strap
3 cm buckles	4 off	Medium duty
5 mm eyelets	15 off	Reinforce carrying straps
1.5 metres		Nylon cord
Metal studs	6 off	Reinforce carrying straps
Heavy duty dust bin liner		Waterproofed inner

ALTERNATIVE RUCKSAC

Cutting List

No Seam Allowance

Allow 3 cm for each seam

MAIN SAC BODY

150 × 70 cm	1 off	137 gms P.U. nylon 270 neoprene could be used
150 × 3 cm	Webbing	Carrying straps
3 cm × 1 metre	Nylon tape	Binding pockets
3 cm buckles	2 off	Carrying straps
3 cm buckles	3 off	Lid and pockets
5 mm eyelets	10 off	For draw cord
3 mm metal studs	6 off	Reinforce shoulder straps

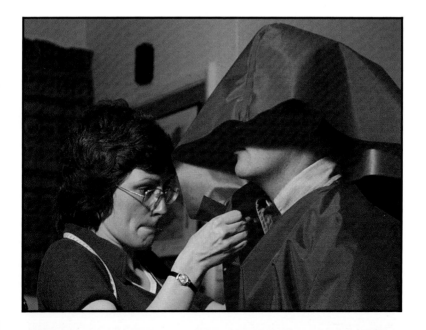

STUFF SACKS FOR SLEEPING BAGS AND OTHER ITEMS

Stuff sacks can be made to any size and you can never have too many stuff sacks for keeping clothing, food or other items when you are out camping or sailing. It is not a bad idea to start by making a few stuff sacks if you have never done any sewing before, because it introduces you to the use of a sewing machine and even if you make a terrible mess of one of these items, you have not destroyed very much fabric.

COMPRESSION BAG

Although I have been making bags of this type for many years, I cannot claim that it is an original design because many other people have made similar things. It is merely a stuff sack strongly made and I always put a lid in it, onto which you sew four hefty nylon straps and buckles. You fold the sleeping bag and put into the bag which is quite big enough to take the sleeping bag easily. Draw the cord round the neck and then by pulling down, tightening on the straps and buckles, you reduce the volume of the sack. Of course you do not reduce the weight, but you reduce the volume which makes it much easier for carrying.

FRAMES FOR RUCKSACS

Rucksacs with external frames seem to have gone out of fashion just now, but I am sure they will be back when people realise that if you are carrying a very large rucksac, the external framed type is certainly very efficient and comfortable to wear. If you wish to make one of these rucksacs, it is quite easy to adapt the pattern for the large day sack to use on an external frame. You merely remove the carrying straps to the frame and sew in strongly, loops of nylon which then hang the rucksac from the frame. A loop from the bottom of the rucksac will hold the bottom of the sack against the frame.

The frames are quite easily made from about 3 cm aluminium tubing which can be bent easily, either with a piece of thick wood with a hole in it or if you have access to one, a proper tube bender.

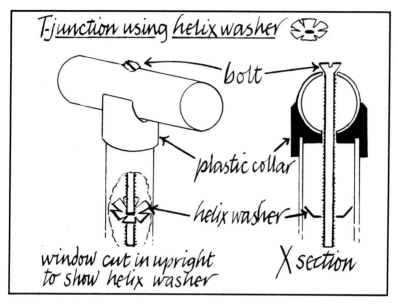

T-junction using helix washer

bolt

plastic collar

helix washer

window cut in upright to show helix washer

X section

FIG. 42

I find tube benders quite common through the increase in Do-It-Yourself plumbing. The shape I'm sure you can conjure or copy from a friend's rucksac. What you need to be able to do is produce T junctions where the cross-bars join the upright. It is very difficult to weld aluminium and unless you have access to a high-tech workshop this will be an impossible task for you. However, we found, through sheer luck, that roofracks are held together by a system that we now use to hold together the frames of the rucksacs.

Figure 42 demonstrates the use of a HELIX WASHER to produce a very strong T junction in aluminium tubing. We found that if you have a tube cutter, which will only cost you two or three pounds, it is very easy to cut the ends of aluminium tubing square. The plastic collar can be bought from a motor spares shop as a spare for DESMO roof-racks, but if they do not keep them, the address of DESMOS is given in the appendix. The only problem you may have is in finding the helix washers, and the address of the manufacturer is also given in the appendix.

I have found that once you have used the helix washers and got the concept of joining two pieces of aluminium tubing in this manner, you begin to make all sorts of things, like camping tables, and so on, using this method.

WATERPROOF OVER-MITTS

Figure 25 shows you the outlines to make a mitt. I make the outers from waterproof material, often using bits of the 2 + 2 neoprene fabric or 68 gms polyurethane coated fabrics in order to make the waterproof outer. If you wish, you can sew strips of leather on to the palm to make it non-slip. You must remember that you are cutting out a left hand and a right hand and a left thumb and a right thumb.

Line up the 15 cm arch on the thumb with the 15 cm arch on the mitt palm and sew them together along this line. Fold the thumb piece, along this line of sewing in half and then sew the two top edges of the thumb piece together. Now put the mitt back on top of the mitt palm and sew all round the edge that is joining the back to the front.

The inner, made with the fibre-pile fabric, is made exactly the same way except that you do not complete the sewing of the back to the front, you leave about 5 cm on the top of the curve unsewn. This is so that you can fit the fibre-pile inner into the outer.

To complete the mitt, turn the fibre-pile inner the wrong way out and turn the waterproof outer the wrong way out and put the outer inside the inner, lining up the thumbs. Sew the two together around the wrist. Pull the inner glove through the hole you have left in the top edge of the fibre pile fabric and turn the outer so that it is the right way out. You can now stuff the fibre pile inner back inside the outer, first sewing by hand the hole you left in the top edge of the inner.

BITS AND PIECES

Figure 26 shows the bum bag which may be made up in a variety of waterproof materials. The zip should be sewn into the top of the back first. The back should then be sewn onto the front and the webbing strap inserted into the 3 cm side pieces. The length of the strap with the buckle you will have to judge to your size.

GAITERS

Figure 27 shows the outline for making gaiters. Although they could cost you £12 or more in the shops; they can be made easily and cheaply from two thirds of a metre of fabric. The total cost will be around £3 depending on which fabric you use.

Cut four pieces to the shape shown in Figure 27, remembering that you want two rights and two lefts. Take one right and one left and pin together down the front seam and use the clear glue technique after pinning the front seam to hold it together while you sew. This front seam is the most important seam in the gaiter and should be stiffened up in some way. I normally stiffen it by putting into the fell seam some plastic-coated garden wire. It is very important that you stiffen up this front seam, because gaiters must be able to stand up by themselves otherwise they are forever slipping down the legs and it is not possible to hold them up in spite of having a draw-cord around the top edge.

On bought gaiters the elastic webbing is sewn on with a special machine, but I find this very difficult because you have to hold the elastic, stretched out, while you sew it. Therefore I suggest that you sew on tunnels of fabric through which you can thread the elastic and merely sew each end to hold it and the tension.

A good stout zip, about 35 cm long, open-ended, can be put in the back, using the techniques described in the anorak pattern.

Gaiters, bought in the shop, normally have a big hook on the front to hook over the front lace of your boots, but if you cannot find these in a good haberdashery I merely sew on a little ring and use some thin nylon cord to tie the front of the gaiter onto the front lace of the boot. You should also have some sort of elastic under the foot to hold the gaiter down.

 # STOP-TOUS

Stop-tous are used in many areas of the world where there are lots of little stones that get thrown up and drop in the top of your boots. Very easily made, they are just a piece of neoprene nylon folded over, top and bottom edge, to take some elastic and a piece of touch and close tape to fasten on each end. They are just therefore, a little gaiter, that goes around the top of the boot.

 # PONCHO CAPE

I have included a pattern for a poncho cape on Figure 28 as many people prefer to walk in the rain wearing a poncho and it is certainly useful if you do any amount of cycling. The make-up is self evident, using a square piece of fabric and folding the edges to make a good strong seam.

 # RAINPROOF LEGGINGS

As a schoolboy we spent our lives cycling everywhere and a cape with a pair of rainproof leggings were a standard uniform in the rain. Rainproof leggings, shown in Figure 29, are very simply made using the pattern for the waterproof overtrousers, only using the legs, and attach them by elastic loops to a belt around the waist.

CYCLIST TYPE CAPE

Figure 30 shows the traditional type cape normally worn by cyclists and which seems to have fallen from fashion, but I see it is making a come-back as cycling is becoming more popular. The make-up is self-evident from the pattern and remember to proof the seams when you have finished and use the anorak pattern when you are putting the hood on the cape.

If you measure your rucksac when it is full and make a box to that size, this can be sewn on to the back of the cape. When you are wearing the cape this box covers your rucksac. This is useful on showery days because it is easy to slip the cape on and off when the rain stops. Four tapes, sewn, one at each corner of the box extension, hold the extension when you are not wearing the rucksac.

NEW ZIP CAPE

Figure 31 shows you a new idea, of making a zipped cape which follows exactly the pattern of the traditional one, but I have put an open-ended zip, the full length of the front of the cape. It seems an attractive garment to wear because on a showery or drizzly day you can open the zip and throw the front of the cape back, thus helping ventilation of your body.

You can, of course, add a box to the back of this cape to cover a rucksac, just as you did with the traditional cape pattern.

Chapter 5

TESTING

I have never come across any mention of testing in traditional books on sewing, but this is understandable as 99% of traditional sewing at home is to make garments for fashion wear and not truly functional garments. Therefore, the strength of the seams, and the like, is not of any great importance to this sort of garment. As we are going to make garments that will be subject to severe stresses in the outdoors, I think we should all understand something of the science of testing fabrics and garments to very high standards. There are many text books on textile testing that would be used by students of textiles in colleges but these, I have found, tend to be rather boring, very technical and difficult to understand, unless you have an "A" level in mathematics. The book listed in our Book List, *Materials and Clothing in Health and Disease* by Renborn and Reese, has a formidable title but you would find it extremely interesting and the section on testing is very readable, although quite detailed.

Most people going into a shop to buy some clothing have just no idea what high levels of technology go into the making, of say, a simple item like a handkerchief. The fibres would be grown or made in factories and then spun into yarn. The simple yarns are likely to have been doubled or twisted together for great strength and undergone several processes before they are made into fabric by weaving or knitting. After weaving the fabrics undergo finishings such as dying, crease-resist and in our particular case, of course, coatings with waterproof material and this industry alone is enormous with a very high level of technology.

In Chapter 2 on Materials we discussed at some length, the different fibres that go into making modern textiles, so in this section we will go on from that and look at the finished fabrics and the end items such as anoraks, tents, etc.

■ YARNS

The fibres will have been spun or made by some other method into a long continuous string-like material that we call a yarn. Of course, the thickness of this yarn can vary enormously and there are three ways of describing how thick this yarn is.

Denier will be familiar to the ladies who buy tights or stockings and are used to asking for different denier nylon which tells them how fine or how thick the tights are going to look. Denier is quite a simple thing, it is just the weight, in grams, of 9,000 metres of the yarn. It is, therefore, called a direct measurement because the higher the denier number, the thicker the yarn will be, for example, 15 denier is a lot finer than 40 denier and so on.

Count. This is an older means of measuring yarns which was started mainly for cotton and wool yarn. It is still used though, and is the number of hanks of yarn which each have 840 yds in them, and the number of these hanks that make a pound in weight. This is an indirect measurement because the higher the count, the thinner the yarn.

Tex. This is a very modern invention which was going to replace all other methods, but as so often happens, just creates a third method of measuring yarns. Although many people use tex, they often quote the equivalent denier or count as well. One tex is the weight in grams of one kilometre of yarn and is therefore a direct method so that the higher the tex number, the thicker the yarn.

Just making the yarn to produce a fabric is in itself an industry with a high level of technology where areas of the country would be concerned with making the fibres, another area is spinning the yarn and even another area where the yarns would be twisted together or doubled in order to make them stronger. Also you would find areas of the country where the yarns after spinning are put onto beams to make them ready for weaving and similar methods to get them ready for knitting.

FABRICS

Men have made fabrics for many thousands of years and there are still in use some very primitive looms which produce very high quality fabrics, because the people who make the fabrics have years and generations of experiences behind them.

There are about 5 different types of fabric that we should look at. Woven, knitted, stretch, bulked and non-woven.

Woven

Woven fabrics are perhaps the commonest type of fabric in the world and certainly one of the earliest produced by man. There are very many different types of weave but they are all based upon having two threads. One, which we call the warp, runs the length of the fabric and a thread on a shuttle, that we call the weft, is ingeniously threaded through the warp threads in a variety of ways. The warp threads running the length of the fabric are numbered and counted and called ends, and the number of ends tells you how many threads per cm in the fabric. The across-wise threads, the weft, are counted and are known as picks, which would tell you the number of threads per cm.

Plain weave fabrics are the oldest and simplest type of woven construction, where the weft yarn is taken over and under alternate warp threads. It is still used to produce poplins for shirtings and raincoats and Oxford weave is used to produce the Ventile fabrics mentioned previously and often for fabrics for anoraks and so on.

A twill weave is commonly used where the pattern of weaving produces diagonal lines in the fabric. Cavalry twill for trousers is well known and this weave is used in gaberdine raincoats, lining fabrics and commonly in denim fabrics for jeans.

Satin weave is used to produce the shiny surface which is not particularly good for abrasion but produces the fabrics required for linings, jackets and other fashion fabrics. A pile weave is of interest to us where large loops are left in the weft fabric which can be cut and made into velvet or velour or even fur fabrics, or left uncut to produce highly absorptive fabrics called terry fabrics that we use for towels and sports shirts etc.

Knitted Fabrics

Knitted fabrics have been increasingly used because knitting is a very efficient sort of operation which is done continuously where weaving is very inefficient because it is a stop/go action where the shuttle is thrown first one way and then the other across the fabric.

Instead of ends and picks, as in weaving, we have wales and courses where a wale is a line of loops running the length of the fabric and courses a line of loops running across the fabric. Most people will be familiar with weft knitting which produces the interlock fabrics that go to make vests and other types of underwear. Warp knitting, however, has been on the increase for many years and produces a fabric much nearer to the look and use of a woven fabric.

Stretch Fabric

Stretch fabrics have always been in great demand for various items, especially stockings and things which need to be worn closely to the body. Nylon itself is a very stretchy fibre and hence the reason stockings are made from nylon and not from other fibres such as terylene which has nowhere near as much stretch within the terylene fibres. Modern technology has given us special chemicals which are made into fibres which are spun especially because they are so stretchy and we have all seen these fibres go into fabrics for tight-fitting trousers and so on for ski-wear and similar outdoor activities.

Bulked-Yarn Fabric

Bulked-yarn fabrics are familiar to us in garments like ski-pants, tights and swim suits, giving not only a stretchy fabric but quite a thick fabric.

Non-Woven Fabric

The expression non-woven material has come into the literature of textiles in recent years, but is in fact a very old term. We could say that paper is a very old form of a non-woven fabric. But we would all be familiar with felt which is perhaps the oldest non-woven fabric, produced from either very poor quality wool or the fur from rabbits and in a wet state was deliberately mangled and pounded when the fibres were literally strung together to produce this very dense and hardwearing material.

The modern non-woven fabrics are made in different ways because with modern fibres becoming soft and soggy when you heat them, it is possible to pound these fibres together and get them to stick and make fabrics that are not woven.

Finishing Fabrics

Even when woven or knitted the fabric is not yet ready for making up into garments or other items of equipment. There are many processes that it will have to go through, each in its own way, with a high level of technology. All fabrics of modern materials will certainly be stabilised in some way after weaving so that they do not move and shrink in the making-up process. Then of course they will have to be dyed or printed in various colours. Crease-resistant, fire-proof and anti-static finishes are just three that may very well be added to fabrics for use in making equipment for outdoor activities.

Flammability of Fabrics

It was difficult to get people interested in the flammability of fabrics. Until recently the authorities showed us how often serious disasters resulting in death came from the burning of settees and chairs filled with modern foams and covered with modern high flammable fabrics. I am afraid we are all to blame for these foams and fabrics going into furniture, because we have just not been willing to pay the extra cost of putting non-flammable finishes onto materials.

■ MEASUREMENT OF FUNCTIONAL PROPERTIES

So we have spun the yarn, woven or knitted the fabric, finished it for some special use and before we make it into anoraks, tents, rucksacs etc, we should like to know a bit about the qualities of this material.

Before we continue, I must make it quite clear that although I am very pleased that you try and make the simple equipment described in the book and try to carry out tests on these fabrics at home, you are not going to be able to claim that they meet British Standards, although most of the tests that we talk about are based upon a British Standard. If you are a student at college or school and want to get really interested in this aspect of fabrics for outdoors, then I suggest that you contact the British Standards Institute at the address given in the Glossary. It would not be a bad idea to contact the Shirley Institute in Manchester, whose

Instrument to measure insulation

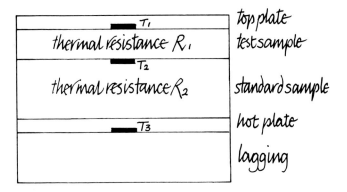

top plate
test sample
standard sample
hot plate
lagging

$$\frac{\text{Insulation } R_1}{\text{Insulation } R_2} = \frac{T_1 - T_2}{T_2 - T_3}$$

Hot plate and test samples ≈ 12" diameter

Measure temperatures T_1 °c
$\qquad\qquad\qquad\qquad T_2$ °c
$\qquad\qquad\qquad\qquad T_3$ °c

Measure thickness of sample
Measure area of sample

Insulation can be measured
with or without top plate

Top plate must be supported
to stop compression of sample

FIG. 43

address is also given, as they are one of the leading test houses in the world and I am sure would be willing to help you. Most good reference libraries will contain copies of the British Standards and these would be well worth reading if you are going to get serious about the topic.

There are about ten tests that we are going to describe, some of which you will be able to carry out and some you will find it quite difficult to make the apparatus and carry out the tests.

Thickness, compressibility and resilience. Most fabrics are very thin materials and you will find it very difficult to measure their thickness accurately. The Shirley Institute make and market a special device called the Shirley Thickness Gauge which is made specially to measure the thickness of fabrics and other materials under a set pressure. We are also interested sometimes in the compressibility and resilience of materials like foams where we are going to use them as a sleeping mat. We want to know how much they are going to compress when we lie on them and, for example, a sleeping bag which has been stuffed into a tiny bag will be compressed and we must be interested in how it will recover its thickness when we use it as a sleeping bag.

Tear strength. This is a measure of how strong a fabric is and it must be of interest to us in the outdoors when we are going to make tents and scuff our trousers and anoraks on rocks, or tear them against thorns or bushes or similar sharp objects. The measurement of tear strength is rather complex and technical and I therefore will leave it for those keen types to look it up for themselves.

Abrasion tests. These tests are carried out on a machine in the laboratory, where a piece of fabric is rubbed by a piece of carborundum paper rather like sandpaper you would use at home, and the number of rubs to produce a hole in the fabric are counted. Although it is carried out in the laboratory and not an exact test for a rubbing that you would give to an anorak or other items, it is known that fabrics can be compared on these machines so that it is possible to say one fabric is better than the other. It would not be difficult if you have a small workshop to make a machine that would carry out these tests for you.

Aesthetic values. Although we are not going to make fashion garments, nevertheless, we are all susceptible to the handle of fabrics and the design of garments. For example, many people just hate the noise of nylon rubbing against nylon when walking along wearing some types of coated nylon fabric anoraks. The measurement of drape and handle of a fabric are still something of a mystery and are difficult to actually measure. One simple test that you can carry out quite easily, is to cut a strip of fabric about 3 cm wide and slide this fabric over the edge of a box say 5 cm high and the length of fabric that you have to push over before the end just reaches the table will give you a good idea of the stiffness of the fabric. You could compare many fabrics in this way. It would be also interesting to test the same fabrics dry and then wet and you might be surprised how much some of them do change under these conditions.

Flammability tests. It is not difficult to carry out flammability tests if you have a fume cupboard at college or school and the Standard tests consist of taking a long strip of fabric and igniting the bottom edge and timing how quickly this strip burns to a set height.

Insulation values. The insulation values of most of the fabrics that we are going to use is not very high, because these fabrics are rather thin and the insulation of any material is very much related to its thickness. The British Standard 4745 describes an apparatus for measuring the thermal insulation of textiles using a very simple system. It would not be difficult for you to make a simplified version of this apparatus in order to measure some insulation values for yourself. The apparatus consists of a plate of metal which is kept warm by electricity and it is usually kept at 33 degrees centigrade as this is the temperature of the skin underneath the clothing. This hot plate is well lagged underneath and round the edges so that heat is only lost upwards. On top of the hot plate is placed a piece of material which has a known and very standard insulation and on top of that the test specimen is put with a cold plate completing the sandwich. To measure the insulation value, you measure the heat lost by the hot plate and this could be done in two ways. First you could measure the electricity required to keep the hot plate at a constant temperature of say 33 degrees centigrade. Or, if you have access to thermistors it would be fairly simple for you to arrange to measure the temperature of the hot plate, the temperature of the top surface of the standard resistance and then the temperature of the outside surface of the test specimen. It is fairly easy mathematically if you know these three temperatures, to work out the amount of heat passing through the test specimen.

In normal physics one usually is measuring the amount of heat passing through some material, but in textiles we want to know the resistance of the material to the passage of the heat. This unit has been given the name Tog which just tells you the amount of heat the fabric or clothing will retain and a full definition of Togs is given in the Glossary. The larger the Tog number the better the insulator so you will see, for example, duvets for beds figures of 9 Tog or 15 Tog or whatever, and the higher this figure the better is the insulator.

Originally the insulation of clothing was measured on people and in this case the units were called CLO and one CLO was the clothing necessary to keep a man in comfort sitting in a room at about 21 degrees centigrade. The clothing represented by one CLO on a man was that of a normal European man dressed in a medium weight suit and shirt and underwear. Although it is much better to measure things on people, this was a very difficult measurement to make and needed a lot of time and complex equipment whereas the Tog is a much more physical measurement on pieces of fabric in a laboratory.

It is possible to measure the insulation of clothing on a man doing various levels of activity in various temperatures and modern electronics has made this much easier, but nevertheless it is still a rather complex procedure and would not be easy for you to carry out unless you had the use of a well established electronic laboratory and access perhaps to a chamber or room that you could keep at a constant temperature.

If it was possible for you to build a piece of equipment described above for measuring Tog value of fabrics and so on, it would be possible to carry out some interesting experiments for yourself, by measuring fabrics when they are wet, when they are damp and when very wet, to show the change in insulation value.

I have kept these last few areas of testing together because they represent looking at the waterproofness of fabrics, which, of course, is one of our prime interests.

Water Repellency
These tests show us mainly what finish has been sprayed onto the outside of a fabric in order that water falling on it will fall off easily and not be absorbed by the fabric.

The spray test consists of spraying water onto a piece of fabric that is mounted tightly in an embroidery ring and put at an angle of 45 degrees. 250 cc of distilled water at 20 degrees centigrade is sprayed onto the fabric from a distance of 15 cm. The specimen is then tapped to remove loose water and given a rating from 1 to 5. One means the fabric is completely wet and 5 means that there is no wetting and no water drops have stuck to the fabric.

The static immersion test. A piece of fabric about 6 to 10 cms square is weighed accurately and immersed in distilled water at 20 degrees centigrade and kept there for 20 minutes. The sample is removed and shaken to remove loose water and re-weighed. The gain in weight is the water absorbed and the lower this figure the better the fabric, as far as we are concerned, in this case. Sometimes this test is done on absorbent fabrics like cotton towellings when the highest absorbency is desired and values of absorbency in excess of 300% can be obtained.

The Bundesmann Test. This is a test regularly used by manufacturers, but one which you will find difficult to carry out yourself because it needs a complex piece of apparatus which consists of four cups on which are mounted four samples of the fabric under test. In each cup underneath the fabric is a spring-loaded arm which wipes round and round under the fabric. During this time the samples are put in the shower of a set rate for ten minutes. After ten minutes the water that has gone through the fabric and collected in each cup is weighed and a figure obtained for the fabric. You would expect to find less than 1cc of water in the cup for a well proofed poplin and 50cc in the cup for a poorly proofed poplin but, of course, the fabrics we are mainly going to use that are coated with a sheet of plastic would not usually admit any water.

Wicking. This test relates to fabrics that we will be wearing next to the skin when we would want the vest or under-garment to wick the sweat away from the skin because the one thing we hate to have is a wet skin. The tests are fairly easy to do and pretty obvious really when you think about it. In the first test a strip of fabric is held vertical with one end in a bowl of distilled water and one measures the height which the water has wicked up the fabric in a given time, say 10 minutes. A dye dissolved in the water makes the observation much easier. In the second test a piece of fabric is held horizontally with just one end dipping into a bowl of water and again the amount of travel of the water along the fabric by wicking is measured over a set period of time.

Hydro-static head test. The hydro-static head test is often quoted to show the waterproofness of a fabric, but was originally invented to measure the waterproofness of non-coated fabrics. The fabrics we are mainly going to use which are coated with polyurethane or neoprene are, of course, almost impervious to water penetration, so the figures that you will get from fabrics like that are just a nonsense because they are so high.

You will see from diagrams in the text that it is quite possible to build a machine for very little money, using a PVC drainpipe and a bit of ingenuity. This simple device will, in effect, measure hydro-static head quite accurately. You are placing a piece of fabric on the machine with the outside surface downwards towards the water, and putting water into the machine under pressure. You measure the height of water that needs to be put into the machine for the second drop to come through the fabric.

The hydro-static head pressure of 100 centimetres is quite adequate for a fully waterproof fabric. If however, you are going to kneel in water or sit in water as you might on a boat, then perhaps 150 centimetres might be better. If you put a sample of fabric on, which is from a showerproof jacket, for example, the terylene cotton mackintosh that you might buy from one of the big stores to wear with your best suit, then you will get a figure of about 50 centimetres.

As the piece of equipment described in the text does not destroy the piece of fabric under test, it is of value because you can take an old anorak and put a piece of the fabric on the machine and test whether you still have retained a full waterproof figure in your anorak. Also you could take say, the neck seam from an anorak and put this across the middle of the test equipment and check that the seams are still waterproof. I can tell you from experience that testing the seams of a cheap thin PU-coated nylon anorak made in Hong Kong, I got a value of 2 or 3 centimetres hydro-static head which means that the water is just going to pour in through those seams.

■ WATERPROOF TESTER (HYDROSTATIC HEAD)

There is an official British Standard Test for Hydrostatic Head in proofed fabrics but, of course, to meet this test you must have the approved equipment which will cost perhaps £1,000. With the device shown in the text you can measure the "waterproofness" of fabrics or seams, that is for all intents and purposes the hydrostatic head figure. This means that you measure the pressure of water that a fabric or seam will stand before the *second drop* goes through.

Equipment
The machine is made from standard 6 cm diameter (or 8 cm or whatever you have) PVC drainpipe and some fitments:–

107 cm of 6cm pipe
10 cm of 6 cm pipe
10 cm of 6 cm pipe
1 Elbow for 6 cm pipe
1 T-piece for 6 cm pipe
1 End cap for 6 cm pipe
1 Tap
18 cm Jubilee clip
1 piece of foamed neoprene 3 cm × approx. 20 cm
1 piece of clear plastic tube 1 metre × 1½ cm diameter
2 Elbows to fit plastic tube
1 metre ruler
1 piece of small bore plastic tube

Test
The test is carried out with the fabric fastened tightly to the top of the neoprene with the Jubilee clip.

Fabric has Outside Downwards
That is, the outside of the fabric is in contact with the water.

The small bore plastic tube (I used a piece from an aerosol can), has been glued in a hole through the neoprene collar with the end level with the top of the collar. This ensures that air is not trapped under the fabric.

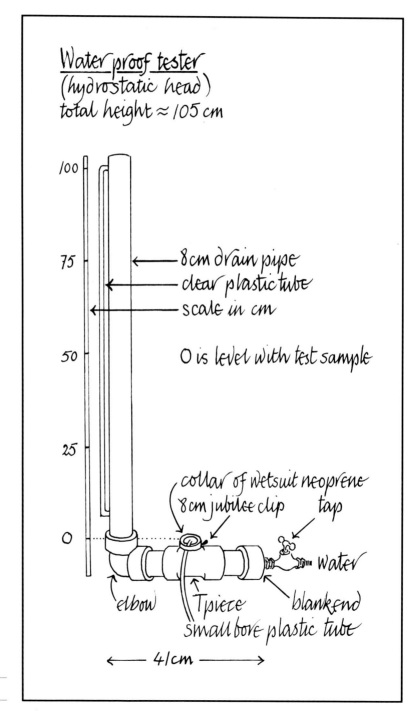

Water proof tester
(hydrostatic head)
total height ≈ 105 cm

100

75 ← 8cm drain pipe
← clear plastic tube
← scale in cm

50 O is level with test sample

25

collar of wetsuit neoprene
8cm jubilee clip   tap
O
Water
elbow   Tpiece   blankend
small bore plastic tube
← 41cm →

FIG. 44

Water is let into the equipment, with a sample fastened tightly by the Jubilee clip, by opening the tap.

Watch the fabric for the second drop to appear and note the level of the water on the scale beside the plastic tube when this drop appears.

So for each sample you will have a result – cm (or inches) of water – which is the *Hydrostatic Pressure* for that sample.

Results

Waterproof fabric should give a result of about 100 cm and a *showerproof fabric* (i.e. a fashion coat) about 40 cm. A cheap anorak with poor seams may only give a figure of 10 cm across the seam. Any modern coated fabric should be able to tolerate 150 cm (60 in) of pressure when new, but after some wear you may well find a big drop in the results.

Electronic waterproof testing. This is an entirely original idea for testing the waterproofness of fabrics and garments. Where the Bundesmann test, if you remember, shows us how much water has passed through a fabric when we poured rain onto a piece under test, this piece of apparatus described now tells you how long it is before water begins to come through the test fabric. It consists of a piece of printed-circuit board which would be put underneath the fabric and then a small box of electronics containing a clock which would, when the water penetrates through the fabric, stop the clock. Thus giving us a recording for the time taken for the first drops of water to come through the fabric. For anyone with any sort of electronic facilities the circuit is quite easy to make and use. If you have access to quite a good electronics laboratory, it might be possible for you to get flexible printed-circuits which are printed onto a thick flexible plastic. If you can obtain this type of circuit it could be put into a garment say, on the shoulder of an anorak, and used outdoors for real to check the time taken for rain to come through your anorak or jacket. This would be a very valuable test to do because you are actually doing it on a person walking in the rain. With all tests of this type, the greatest difficulty is to make rain, because rain is always near zero degrees centigrade when it falls in Britain and it is very difficult to get the right

Electronic waterproof tester

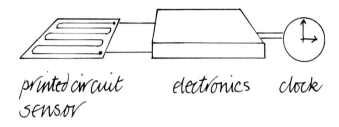

printed circuit   electronics   clock
sensor

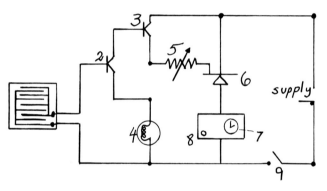

supply

1. sensor - elements 1 mm apart
2.⎫ pair of
3.⎭ matched transistors
4. indicator lamp
5. sensitivity adjuster
6. thyristor
7. clock
8. light and/or buzzer
9. switch

FIG. 45

droplet size to imitate the different types of rain. What you must have if you are going to try and create rain seriously, is to have a high tower, as high as possible, but certainly 10 metres or more, so that the water has time to fall and get into smallish droplets.

Water vapour permeability. Of all the tests connected with waterproof fabrics, this is the most contentious of all and is the one that is currently being developed. There are several methods being used depending upon which company you speak to and the different methods can give wildly differing results for the same fabric. I have seen results from one laboratory 10 times the results from another laborabory, using the same fabric but their own test. If you wish to do simple tests of water vapour permeability yourself, it is quite easy to make the equipment in its simplest form. You will need small dishes about 8 cms across, onto which you can stick or fasten in some way the samples of fabric so they are tightly held on the neck of the dish. You are going to weigh the dish empty, put water into it, put the fabric on the top, seal the fabric round and leave the dish for at least 24 hours in a controlled cabinet or room. When you weigh the dish again it will have lost weight and the only way it can lose weight is by evaporating the water through the fabric. This gives us a measure of the water vapour permeability which is normally given as grams per square metre of fabric in 24 hours. One of the problems is that you really want the level of water right up next to the fabric but not touching it, because if you have a gap between the fabric and the top of the water, this represents a barrier to the evaporation of the water. If you develop a routine for yourself for each test, then the figures you get will not be accurate to the nearest tenth gram but you will certainly be able to test different fabrics and say that one is better than the other. I do not believe that the controversy over water vapour permeability of a fabric is going to be a vital component of a good waterproof jacket, because I think that the design of the jacket will be equally important.

Climate – Weather – Environment?

If you are going to be seriously involved with the design of clothing and equipment for expeditions, you will have to learn a little about the weather, climate, and environment. I am sure that if you only want to go on expeditions or just make some equipment for expeditions and not necessarily test the equipment, then you must still know about the weather.

When testing equipment that you have designed and made, you will need to measure and record the conditions of the environment where you carried out the tests. The records that you keep for this purpose will be slightly different from the records kept by the Meteorologists. Let us look at the meaning of the various words.

Climate and Weather

The two words have similar meanings and both relate to conditions outdoors. Climate represents the average of temperature, rain, sunshine, etc over many years. For example, we know that the climate of the UK varies between 5°C in January to 18°C in June with 60 cm of rain per year. We call this Temperate Climate. We classify other parts of the globe with similar climate as Desert, Tropical, Arctic etc.

Weather is the climate that we are experiencing now. Therefore, we have a Weather Forecast which will, we hope, predict the conditions that we will experience over the next 24–36 hours.

The Meteorological Office

The "Met" office is a Government funded service. It records the weather all over the world from land based laboratories, from ships at sea, from balloons in the sky and most recently from satellites orbiting the earth.

The "Met" office at Bracknell, Berks, stores all the information on huge computers. From this they make the weather predictions.

It is possible to get the "Met" office readings of the weather for your district. If you are going to try experiments on the equipment you have designed and made, when worn by people outdoors, you will need to record the local conditions for yourself.

You must record the conditions where you are working and not rely on a "Met" station 20 miles away.

You will also find that although the "Met" office records many different climatic factors, they are not quite the factors that we wish to know for testing equipment.

The frustrating aspect of trying to test equipment outdoors, is the weather. Try to arrange for your subjects, equipment and test equipment to be together and then choose a date for the experiment, i.e., to test a waterproof jacket, then you wait for the rain.

If you are trying to organise a Church Bazaar, outdoors, you can say any Saturday and know that it will rain that day. If we try to organise a clothing trial for waterproof jackets we immediately get a drought.

So we find that any large concern, such as the Ministry of Defence or large private firms who have a major interest in testing clothing or equipment, in the end build Climatic Chambers. At the turn of a switch (and a very expensive switch) they can simulate (more or less copy) any climate in the world.

These chambers exist but have disadvantages. First, they never produce all the conditions that you require.

Second, they are limited in size so that if you are designing a large ship, tank or aircraft there are very few chambers large enough to accommodate such large objects.

Third is a psychological factor rather than a physical one. Let us pretend that we must select a team to go to Mount Everest. It is expensive to take everybody out to Mount Everest but it is possible to find a chamber that can provide us with the conditions, $-40°C$, high winds, hard exercise and an altitude of 29,000 ft. We put our candidates through the chamber and test their reactions etc. But there is one very big difference. If you feel ill in the chamber you put up your hand and some kind doctor comes into the chamber and takes you out! If you feel ill on Everest and put up your hand, I am afraid nothing happens. You must just battle it out yourself.

This type of selection where we simulate (or imitate) conditions is used in selecting people for many jobs – obviously in jobs like pilots, SAS, where we can never use "real" conditions of danger, but also in more routine jobs like firemen, teachers, coal miners, and even executives, where we can never give a candidate the real stress of his or her job.

Of course chambers have real value in helping selection, training and testing equipment where the equipment does not know the difference between Everest and the chamber.

What to Measure?

Temperature
How hot or cold is the environment is the first and obvious factor, but it must be measured properly. When the Met Office say we will get a temperature of 20°C, this is the AIR temperature measured in a shaded tube. That is a SHADE temperature. The air temperature may be 20°C but if you measure the roof of a black car in the sun, you can read 60°C or 70°C.

Traditionally the air temperature was measured with an aspirating psychrometer. A clockwork or electric fan sucked air at a standard rate over the bulb of a thermometer held in a metal tube – chromium plated to reflect the sun. There were normally 2 thermometers – one to get the air temperature (shade) and another thermometer with a cotton sock on the bulb. The cotton was wet with distilled water and would read a temperature lower than the DRY bulb due to evaporation of the water. This is the WET bulb temperature and tells us how much moisture is in the air, that is HUMIDITY.

Thermistors

For many years mercury thermometers (and occasionally alcohol-filled for low temperatures) were the only easy method of measuring temperature and are still widely used.

Modern electronics has given us other methods of measuring temperature. Tiny specks of material are connected to very fine wires. The electrical resistance of the speck changes with temperature so by measuring the resistance you know the temperature. The speck is known as a thermistor and the apparatus as an electro-thermometer, which now usually gives a digital read-out.

The advantage of an electro-thermometer when you go outdoors to test equipment are obvious – they are not fragile like glass, they are very small and if you wish to leave a piece of equipment for days in the field a recorder will read the temperature for you every minute, every hour or any interval that you choose.

I have not included any circuit diagrams for electro-thermometers because they are in common use in school and college laboratories. If you are going to construct electro-thermometers you will need 3 types for our purpose. First, you need instruments that can measure a wide range of temperatures, say $-20°C$ to $70°C$, that need only to be accurate to $0.5°C$ to measure the temperature of the environment. Then you need an instrument that can measure say $0°C$ to $40°C$, accurate to about $0.25°C$ to measure the temperature of the clothing and skin of the subject. Finally, you will need instruments to measure the body temperature of the subject which need only to cover $30°C$ to $40°C$ but must be accurate to $0.1°C$.

Probes

With thermistors the active speck is so small that it can be made into many shapes by resin. One most useful setting for clothing experiments is the use of a large hypodermic needle. The thermistor is set, in resin, at the sharp end of the needle which has been blunted on a grindstone. The needle is still sharp enough to be pushed through clothing to measure the temperature of the clothing layers underneath and even the skin temperature can be measured.

Humidity

The measurement of humidity is the most difficult of all to make and the control of humidity in buildings is the most difficult factor to control in air conditioning plants.

We have mentioned above the Wet and Dry temperatures which are the most common way to estimate humidity. Charts are available that show the Humidity if you know the Wet and Dry temperatures. If you do not have an Aspirating Hygrometer then a simpler device to make is a Sling Hygrometer. Two thermometers – Wet and Dry are put in a sling that looks just like a football rattle. This is whirled round the head but is not as satisfactory as the Aspirating Hygrometer.

Definitions

We must now be a little Scientific and look at four words used to describe Humidity.

Absolute Humidity

The amount of water that air can hold depends on the temperature of the air (and the pressure). If we take 1 cubic metre of air –
At −20°C it holds 0.892 gms of water as vapour
At 0°C it holds 4.835 gms of water
At 30°C it holds 30.039 gms
This is Absolute Humidity and can be given as gms per cubic metre of air at a given temperature.

The Absolute Humidity can also be quoted as a pressure. Air pressure can be measured with a barometer and is about 760 mm of mercury. The pressure of the air is a total of all the different gases in air – oxygen, nitrogen etc and as water vapour is a gas this also exerts a pressure depending on how much there is present.

Relative Humidity

Humidity is usually quoted as Relative Humidity, that is as a percentage. This figure is meaningless unless you also quote the temperature.

Above we have said that air at 30°C can hold 30.039 gms of water as water vapour. If we have some air at 30°C and we measured the water vapour and found 30.039 gms per cubic metre that would be 100% Relative Humidity. If we took air at 30 degrees C.

and only found 25 gms of water vapour that would be 83% of
30.039, that is the air has a Relative Humidity of 83%.

Dewpoint
If we take some air which has some water vapour in it and we cool
the air slowly, at a certain temperature we see a mist form as some
of the water vapour condenses out to become droplets of water.
We have all seen this when we breathe on to a cold mirror. It is
possible to get a heated mirror which does not cloud over when
our hot wet breath hits the glass.

It is possible to measure the temperature when the water just
starts to condense. This is called the DEWPOINT, it is a very
accurate method but mainly used by physicists in laboratories.

This point – the Dewpoint – where water changes from a gas to a
liquid water, is of great importance in clothing especially in
designing waterproof clothing.

You put on a thin anorak because it looks like rain, you keep
walking and build up a layer of warm air under the anorak that is
pretty well saturated with water vapour (from you) and is say
30°C. Then it rains, rain is always near 0°C in the UK, the
temperature of the thin fabric drops to say 5°C almost instantly –
the air at 30°C could hold 30 gms of water, air at 5°C can only
hold about 6 gms – 24 gms of water suddenly appears on the
INSIDE of your anorak – you have crossed the Dew-Point of the
air at 30°C and the water just drops out. Many people return a
new anorak swearing that it has leaked when they have just had
instant condensation.

Let us take one example:

In Bahrain we get the world maximum humidity, although many
people think that the record is held by Burma.

Bahrain Island. Very hot humid.

Dry bulb–Shade–Temperature 38°C.
Wet bulb–Shade–Temperature 36.5°C.
Relative Humidity 90%
Dewpoint 30°C

Absolute Humidity 37 mm Hg Pressure
Sunshine 1140 Watts per sq metre.

For every sample of air these five results could be measured.

This is a fearsome climate in which to live but to which people have managed to adapt to over many thousands of years without air-conditioning. Of course, these conditions do not happen every day. These are the maximum temperatures that are recorded for short periods each year.

Relative Humidity is the most used result in experiments with clothing as our thermal comfort is largely influenced by the Relative Humidity.

For example, in the desert, the Shade Air Temperature can be 50°C but the Relative Humidity can be as low as 5%. You will be sweating at a high rate but because the air is so dry the sweat evaporates immediately and you have a dry skin.

In Bahrain the shade temperature will only be 35°C but the Relative Humidity is 85–90%. Your sweat rate will be very high and the high humidity in the air means that the sweat does not evaporate easily. So you sweat more and always you have a wet skin. Nowadays, many buildings will be air-conditioned to about 20°C. After several hours in this air-conditioned atmosphere your skin will be quite cool and not sweating. Now when you emerge into the humid air outside your skin is instantly wet, not with sweat, but condensation from the air. Your skin has cooled below the Dewpoint of the outside air.

Radiation

We have made equipment to measure the Shade Air Temperature and the Met. Office never give the temperature in the "Sun". The problem that the final temperature of objects in the sun depends on the amount of sunshine obviously but equally on the "colour" of the object.

Physicists speak of a "BLACK BODY" which absorbs all the energy falling on it. "Black" does not really refer to the artist colour black, but means that all energy is absorbed. Let me illustrate the point with a simple experiment. On a bright sunny day, preferably with little or no wind, go round parked cars and if you can measure the temperature of the car roofs you will find that black cars are the hottest and truly white cars quite a bit cooler. I can guarantee though that blue, grey, green etc will be almost as hot as black.

The heating effect of radiation is of great importance if you have to provide clothing for special jobs like firemen, steel furnace workers etc where they face very hot objects.

The opposite of a black body is a perfect reflector. A mirror is a perfect reflector (almost) of light but not for radiation. The best reflector of infra-red radiation is polished silver which reflects about 98% of infra-red rays. We do not use silver to reflect an electric fire because the silver soon becomes tarnished – so we use chromium plate which reflects 95%. More about infra-red radiation is given in Chapter 7.

Black Globe

To measure the effect of the heat from the sun we use a metal globe about 15 cm in diameter. A float from a cistern was ideal but now they are made in plastic and not so good but I am sure that using a plastic float you can make a metal sphere.

Paint the globe matt black and put a thermometer or thermistor at the centre. The temperature in the black globe is the temperature of the air plus the effect of the sun. The globe temperature could be lower than the air temperature if you have a large cold source, for example, in an ice cave.

Wind

An anemometer is the instrument to measure the speed of wind. Usually it is 4 cups spinning round a central point. These items are now easily available thanks to the expansion of yachting

Rain

The amount of rain is measured by catching rain in a funnel over a timed period.

To make rain is not easy. To get the right size of drops falling at the right speed at near zero degrees centigrade is more difficult than you think. The only way seems to have quite a high tower – at least 10 metres high.

If you want to make rain in the laboratory for use with the electronic detector described in the text, dropping water through a fine mesh can be used.

Sweat Loss

If you are going to try experiments on people wearing different clothes, and I presume these will be largely carried out in the UK, then you will have to measure the sweat loss of people.

What we need is the "nude" weight of subjects before and after – this was quite difficult until recently, there being no scales that would weigh a human weight accurately. When I investigated the market the only scales that could weigh a man to about a quarter of a pound was made in Denmark for weighing pigs.

The scales used to weigh jockeys were hopelessly inaccurate and the best bathroom scales would not weigh you within a pound. How then can some of my friends claim that they have lost half a pound? The answer is in the mind! Now with modern electronics it is possible to buy scales that are electronic and not mechanical which are quite accurate.

Human Subjects

Although I hope that you will try some of the laboratory tests described in the text, I always find that the experiments using human subjects are the most interesting. These experiments can also produce quite original results, especially if you can measure some of the factors like skin temperature, body temperature, sweat rate, etc.

Of course you would also have a questionnaire to get a measure of the opinions of subjects.

Beware of the judgement of people, they are quite fickle. Give them A & B, today they choose A and tomorrow B. If you are giving subjects a questionnaire you should try to design the experiment so that the subject does not know which garment they are wearing! It is all too easy to choose garment A if you know that it is the £150 model.

I was pleased when watching a children's TV programme recently to see that they had a simple device to stop children knowing which (shoes) they were wearing during a trial. A large circle of card was fastened round the neck of the children so that it was impossible to see their feet.

Medical Approval
Finally, we must be careful with any experiment using human subjects. You should have a carefully planned schedule which should be approved by a friendly doctor!

You should really draft a letter for each subject to sign saying that they are willing to take part in the experiment.

It is not a good idea to use children, that is anyone under 16 years old – they cannot consent to take part in experiments.

This sounds as if you might conduct experiments that might lead to an accident with serious consequences. I hope you will not try experiments that could be dangerous, but even the simplest experiment can go wrong – so just be sensible.

A Simple Routine
I do hope that some people will develop experiments and carry out some complex tests or experiments on clothing and equipment, but really interesting results can be obtained with simple routines and equipment.

This routine was developed when a large high street store asked me to help with improvements in the "waterproofness" of their coats. The results of this simple experiment were responsible for a major change in designs for this large company.

We had 17 different "shower proof jackets" which were for the female customer. Luckily I had a "rain" shed but you could easily make a simple rain device (or wait for a wet day) which will give you a heavy shower – say 3 cm rain in one hour.

The coats were fashion garments so I decided that they should protect the wearer for 15 minutes in rain at 3 cm per hour. This represents shopping in a heavy shower.

I had them walk round in the rain shed for 15 minutes on a cool day with minimum clothing so they would not sweat. The subjects were female and wore a cotton T-shirts with sleeves and whichever jacket they were testing.

We weighed the test jacket before and after, we weighed the T-shirt before and after. The two sets of results give the final comparison we were looking for, that is:

How much water did the jacket absorb?

How much water went through the jackets?

We have 17 different "shower" proofed coats (not all made by the sponsor and two were very expensive) and with this simple routine we found the following conclusions.

Conclusions
Only one jacket passed the test of 15 minutes in rain at 3 cm per hour. This jacket was a showerproof terylene cotton, like several other coats under test, but passed the test because the designer had put a short cape around the shoulders.

Several jackets leaked but the leakage was so small that perhaps it was acceptable?

One jacket, made and sold by the sponsor, was so bad that the subject gave up after 6–7 minutes as she was saturated. The main reason for this saturation was that the seams were sewn with cotton thread (and not sealed) which wicked the rain through, this water was then spread rapidly right through the inside of the coat by the knitted cotton backing. The jacket was a "leather" look fabric with knitted cotton base fabric. I was amazed that

this firm had sold thousands of jackets but had never had one
returned because it leaked.

Statistics

If you are into statistics of course you should plan the experiments
and work out all the significant factors, but I am not going to put
off the non-mathematical readers. In any event those into statistics
will know how to design the experiments. You can carry out
many experiments which can produce valid results without the
mathematical analysis.

HOW CLOTHES
AFFECT
YOUR BODY

As a scientists I should call this chapter, Human Physiology, or the Biochemistry of Human Function. However, I felt that such a pompous title might deter many people from reading it. A human physiologist is interested in how the normal human body functions, whereas a doctor tends to be more interested in the body when it is not functioning properly, although of course certain aspects of disease help us to understand how the normal body does function.

MAMMALS

Humans belong to the group of animals with backbones that we call mammals and they range from a minute mouse to a whale weighing several hundred tons. You need three qualifications to be a mammal. One, you must keep your body temperature constant; two, you must have hair on your skin; and three, you must produce milk to suckle your young offspring. These three qualifications developed over millions of years and some of the early mammals had the qualifications rather poorly developed. The particular qualification we are looking at is keeping your body temperature constant and there are mammals alive today, in Australia especially, who do not keep their body temperature as constant as we do and of course there are mammals like bears who, in the winter, go into a deep cave and go into a very deep sleep that we call hibernation, when their body temperature drops quite considerably and helps to see them through the long winter. The advantage which keeping a constant body temperature gave to mammals was that they could live throughout the world and function over a very wide range of climates when other animals like reptiles could not move when the temperature dropped. You can see quite clearly that if an insect is put in a fridge, very quickly it literally cannot move because it is just too cold, but when you bring it out and let it warm it will fly off just as it did before. Even big reptiles like crocodiles or snakes have to sun themselves to get warm in the mornings so that they can move quickly to hunt for food.

◼ DEEP BODY TEMPERATURES

We all know the importance of our body temperature, because if you are ill the first thing a doctor does is to stuff a thermometer into your mouth and then proceed to ask you questions which you cannot answer because your mouth is full of thermometer! The temperature given on the thermometer you will find is remarkably constant although there are small variations between night and day and of course if you have been doing violent exercise then your temperature will be slightly raised. Very few diseases seem to lower the body temperature, but many diseases do raise the body temperature and this is a good indication to the doctor of the cause of your illness.

So humans have a body temperature of 98°F or 37°C if taken under the tongue for several minutes. To tell you exactly what deep body temperature means is not easy. It roughly means that the temperature of the blood circulating in your body is kept at this constant temperature and any small change like 0.5°C is certainly felt by us. However, you would find that areas of the body might be hotter than 37°C such as the surface of the liver when it is active in processing our body products.

◼ THERMAL COMFORT

The easiest way to explain this constant temperature of our body is to talk about thermal comfort which is the state we live in most of the time. Thermal comfort means that your body temperature taken by a thermometer in the mouth is normal, that is 37°C. If you measure the temperature of your skin all over your body and made an average of that, you would find that it is 33°C which is about 92°F. Equally important you would find that there is only about 3°C or 4°C between the temperature of the skin on different parts of your body and that you prefer that your chest and belly are warmer than your hands and feet. It is the temperature of our skin that tells us the day to day running of our body. So if you are sitting watching television and there is a large open window, or for some other reason you start to feel chilly, it means that the average of your skin temperature has dropped from 33°C to perhaps 32°C or 31°C and automatically you would get up and put on a cardigan, put another bar on the electric fire or shut the window. Or if you sense that you are a bit warm you would do the opposite.

 WATER LOSS

Even when you are sitting at thermal comfort watching television you are still losing body fluids by two means. First, as you breathe out you are breathing out water vapour into the air and although this is not important for clothing, it is important if you are sleeping in a tent as each person in the tent will blow out into the air about one litre or two pints of water over a night's sleep. Second, although you are not sweating, you are still losing fluid through your skin because the skin is not completely waterproof. We call this kind of water loss insensible sweating because you have no control over it. The loss of body liquid through your skin is about 300 cc in 24 hours.

 TEMPERATURE CONTROL

If you take a milk bottle or a flask, or some other container and fill it with water at 38°C and leaving a thermometer in the water, stand the flask on a bench, you will see that the temperature of the water rapidly goes down. There are very few places in the world where the temperature of the water would not drop from 38°C because most places in the world are cooler than 38°C. In Europe where the temperature, even in the summer, could only be 20°C or so, the water in the flask would rapidly cool. So if this represents your body we must keep adding heat to the water in order to keep the temperature constant. Of course if you put plastic foam round the bottle as we put clothes on ourselves, you will delay the fall in temperature for a while but eventually unless you are adding heat, the water temperature will drop. It would not be difficult for you to make a small heater with a thermostat on, plugged into the electricity supply which would switch on and off and keep the temperature of the water at 38°C and this is precisely what we have inside our head, a thermostat.

HUMAN THERMOSTAT

Inside our brain we have a complex mechanism which controls the temperature of our body very precisely and it controls a very sophisticated system which, being a living system, is always on the move, that is it is a dynamic system. So as a person you are moving about, you are eating food which has to be digested, you are changing from one temperature to another and so on and so it has to be a very complex system of control. We spend most of our lives with our deep body temperature remarkably constant and we do this using the very smallest blood vessels in our body called capillaries of which there are many millions. These are situated in great numbers just underneath our skin. If we are getting just a bit too warm we can open up some of these blood vessels and pump more of the warm blood up to the skin where it cools off, or if we are feeling a bit chilly we can reduce the amount of blood circulating in the skin and so reduce the amount of heat we are losing. We have all witnessed this as we appear quite pink and flushed after a hot bath or shower and appear much paler when we are cold in the winter. Let us now look at what happens when we get more seriously hot or cold.

GETTING HOT

I think it is fair to say that there are many more people in the world acclimatised or used to heat than cold. Even Eskimos get used to the heat when they are in igloos. We think man must have come from a tropical country because we are much better at keeping cool in the heat than warming ourselves up in the cold. Let us now imagine that our brain senses that we are getting too warm and our body temperature is starting to rise. While we do all the things that we have mentioned, we open the window, take off some clothes or some other action like that, if our body temperature keeps on going up our brain senses this and now invokes our highly successful and extremely efficient system of cooling. All over our body, although not equally spaced, there are $2\frac{1}{2}$ million little glands coming out onto the surface of our skin that we call sweat glands. We have a very accurate control over the amount of sweat that comes out of these glands. There are just a few people who have been born without sweat glands and although they can live comfortable lives in Northern Europe, they would find extreme difficulty in going to the tropics. The sweat glands produce this fluid and it spreads out over the skin where, when it evaporates, it cools the skin down and so removes heat from the body. Sweat is a very complex liquid which contains salt and many other body chemicals. The sweating mechanism only works if the liquid sweat that we have put onto the skin can evaporate and if it cannot evaporate, as happens when we put on a waterproof jacket, then cooling does not take place. Or if we are in parts of the world where humidity is very high once again the sweat cannot evaporate and we just get hotter. Of course in Victorian times when prudery was much to the fore, the saying was that horses sweat, men perspire and ladies glow, trying to indicate that it was below a lady's dignity to sweat. This is not the case and both sexes are quite equally capable of sweating. Most people do not appreciate the amount of sweat that can be produced, especially if one is in a hot dry climate where the sweat evaporates almost as soon as it is produced and so you never feel the skin wet. Going to somewhere like the Persian Gulf where the climate produces the worst heat stress in the world, the humidity is so high that one of the problems Europeans face is having a

constantly wet skin which we do not like psychologically. The
amounts of sweat that can be produced have been recorded
scientifically and it is quite easy to produce 2 litres of sweat per
hour. That is 4 pints of sweat which has been recorded in people
working in furnaces and so on and has also been recorded in the
Persian Gulf. Of course these are extreme figures but it is quite
easy for you to lose 500 cc, that is one pint of sweat in an hour.

You will rapidly dehydrate if you carry on sweating at this rate.
The danger of dehydrating is that the brain senses that we are
losing masses of fluid and begins to reduce the sweat rate so that
you will then get hotter than you should be. Therefore, if you are
going to a hot climate or you are going to do violent exercise where
you will be losing a lot of sweat, it is very important that you
drink fluid before you sweat. Once you are thirsty you are starting
to dehydrate. I am sure many of you will be thinking this chap is
mad because I am never going to go into the desert of the Persian
Gulf, I am going to do a Duke of Edinburgh's Award Scheme
Expedition in Britain or Northern Europe. What you must
remember is that when you are walking in Britain on a warm
summery day and it is raining, you have put yourself into a
climate very similar to that of the Persian Gulf. You have to put on
a waterproof jacket which has covered quite a large area of your
body with a waterproof layer. You are working hard walking up
hill, so you are producing a lot of heat from moving your muscles
and thus your body temperature begins to rise, your brain senses
the rise and starts to sweat. But of course the sweat cannot
evaporate because of the waterproof jacket and you produce more
sweat and it is quite easy walking in the mountains on a warm
rainy day, wearing a waterproof jacket, and whether it is made
from a breathable material or a conventional material for you to
lose a remarkable amount of sweat. I hope you do not think that
I am saying that when you are walking in the summer in Britain
and it is raining you should take off your waterproof jacket. One
true statement is that you can never be as wet with your own
sweat as you can be wet with rain. If you walk in the rain without a
waterproof jacket you will rapidly get saturated and start to cool
down and be in great danger. One British tradition of making a
brew of tea or other liquid when you stop for the day is a very
good piece of advice, because you will find if you are thirsty you

are never hungry. If then you have a brew of tea and drink two or three cups of tea you will suddenly find you are ravenously hungry.

As sweat contains quite a large amount of salt, people often ask about taking salt tablets or drinking salt drinks. It is true to say that workers in steel factories are often given salt beer by their employers in order to replace the sweat they are losing. But for most people replacing the fluid by any drink whether it is milk, water, tea or coffee is far more important than replacing the salt. British cooking on the whole is very salty and we consume far more salt than we ever need. It has been found with excess sweating it is possible to lose salt which if not replaced will cause "boilermaker's cramp" which was experienced by people in steel factories and various other hot places if they did not replace the salt. "Heat stroke" and "sunburn" are often mistaken for each other but do often occur together. Heat stroke is a complex medical condition when someone has been in a very hot place and not been able to get cool and needs medical attention quickly. It is often associated with sunburn because the person has often suffered the heat stroke through lying, with very few clothes on, on a hot beach. Sunburn is not related to the temperature but to the amount of ultra-violet light you receive from the sun which can penetrate the skin and you literally have been burnt. The dangers of this are now made apparent in the press.

GETTING COLD

Rather like the response to heat, we have two systems to respond to cooling. One that we use all the time unconsciously when there are small changes in temperature and one that we only invoke when cooling is more serious.

MILD COOLING

If we are sitting in our state of thermal comfort and for some reason the climate around us changes by having a draught from an open window, the sun going in or some other reason, we change the amount of blood that we pump to the capillaries under the skin. Thus reducing or increasing the heat lost by the blood. We do this unconsciously all the time to keep ourselves in the state of thermal comfort and of course as humans we have other means to adjust our thermal comfort by putting on, or taking off, clothes or increasing the heat from the fire or similar means. We judge all this by the average temperature of our skin because during these everyday changes, our body temperature is not being altered.

SERIOUS COOLING

If we are in a position where our body continues to cool and the changes in blood flow to the skin etc are not sufficient to stop the cooling then we invoke our second mechanism, when our body temperature has dropped half a degree Centigrade or one degree Farenheit. We call this mechanism shivering, which means the brain send impulses to the muscles for them to work not by moving limbs but by rippling movements, burning the glucose in the muscles and so producing heat. Of course shivering is moving muscles so it is a very tiring process and unfortunately is not a very efficient process in itself. When we shiver the muscles burn glucose and produce by-products which unfortunately for us as they circulate in the blood, cause the capillaries in the skin to open up. So we lose some of the heat we have produced by sending this blood to the surface where it is cooled. We have all experienced shivering because we do not need to drop our deep body temperature necessarily to shiver for a few seconds. Going from a hot room suddenly outdoors with little clothing on can produce this shivering mechanism. However, if you are shivering for more than half a minute or so, you should be aware and take some sort of action because your body is telling you that it is cooling down. However often have I seen some irate mum at the swimming pool or the seaside where little Johnny has been in splashing in the cold sea, come out and is now standing and shivering for all his might, being shouted at by the irate mum to

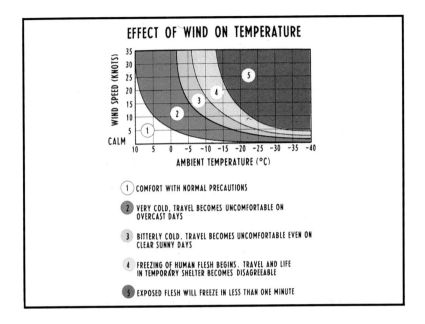

EFFECT OF WIND ON TEMPERATURE

WIND SPEED (KNOTS)

AMBIENT TEMPERATURE (°C)

1 COMFORT WITH NORMAL PRECAUTIONS

2 VERY COLD, TRAVEL BECOMES UNCOMFORTABLE ON OVERCAST DAYS

3 BITTERLY COLD. TRAVEL BECOMES UNCOMFORTABLE EVEN ON CLEAR SUNNY DAYS

4 FREEZING OF HUMAN FLESH BEGINS. TRAVEL AND LIFE IN TEMPORARY SHELTER BECOMES DISAGREEABLE

5 EXPOSED FLESH WILL FREEZE IN LESS THAN ONE MINUTE

stop shivering, as though he can. It is an automatic reaction and she should realise that he is very cold and quickly dry him and get his clothes on and get him warm again. Shivering can produce enormous amounts of heat so that if you are used to the cold, used to shivering, you can produce five or six times the amount of heat you are producing now sitting comfortably reading this book. But you must remember it is a muscle movement and you would find it extremely tiring to shiver for long periods. If you are in some position where cold is extreme and your body keeps on cooling, you will see from the illustration in the text that quickly shivering stops when your body temperature reaches about 32–33°C. When this happens you are in very real danger. You will see from the diagram that if your body temperature drops only a little you will develop the symptoms of confusion, disorientation and introversion. It is quite possible that if you go outdoors in Northern Europe, including Britain, that you may well find yourself in a position like this or have someone in your party in a position like this where they are not suffering but will show some of these symptoms. You must be aware of them and realise that you make wrong decisions, take wrong turns, fall over cliffs and all sorts of other things when your mind is in this state.

We say that you are now in a state of mild hypothermia which just means in Latin, low temperature. In this state your life is not in immediate danger provided you have some means of reducing your heat loss. This means stopping and perhaps putting up a tent or stopping and putting the cold person in a sleeping bag and then in a poly bivi bag provided his clothing is not wet through. If the clothing is saturated in water if possible it must be removed and dry clothing put on and then place them in the sleeping and poly bags. If it is not possible to change the wet clothing, put the patient in the polythene bag first and then in the sleeping bag so that his clothing does not wet the sleeping bag. If you are in this state although your life is not in immediate danger, it can produce fatal results if steps are not taken to retrieve the situation and this state of hypothermia is very common in Britain. Speaking to a friend who is a GP at a well known seaside resort, it is quite common for him to have 20 people brought off the beach in the summer suffering from this state of hypothermia. Often children who have been bathing too long, but more often these days people who have been sailboarding or water-skiing getting repeatedly wet, not realising they are slowly cooling down.

Although on the diagram there are coloured bands showing different states, this does not happen when you are being cooled down. You slip from one state into the other without knowing it. It is a continuous slippery slope and rapidly can get you into serious trouble if steps are not taken to relieve the situation. If people get in a state of serious hypothermia then one must get immediate medical help. If this is impossible they can rapidly slip into a situation where they will just die.

What is difficult to get across to people who are tough he-men mountaineers or members of the forces or similar tough sorts of people, is that no matter how fit, how strong or how experienced you are, if you get in a situation where you are cooling down and your deep body temperature starts falling, when it reaches a certain level, which is not precise but not very low, then you will die no matter who you are. When you get below the introvertion level on the diagram unless you get immediate medical help then your life is in very real danger.

Let us look on the bright side and hope that when you are on a Duke of Edinburgh's Award Expedition none of this happens. Of course, it is quite possible if you go out on the hills you can get very cold and get into one of these extreme shivery states but if you are aware of what is happening to you or someone else then you can take steps to halt it.

COLD HANDS

I have found that text books on human physiology never talk to you about cold hands. If you have ever been in one of these extreme shivery states where you are just beginning to get into hypothermia and you are getting very cold, what you should remember is that not only are your hands very painful but they are often very stiff. Our standard test was to ask someone to open a box of matches, take out a match, and strike the match. You would find this impossible to do when you have cold hands. It has a very real practical implication in that if you were in a liferaft or on the mountains and you had a pack of flares with you, it would be impossible for you to open them and get the flare going before the helicopter had disappeared over the horizon.

Let us look at astronauts. You only need three qualifications to be an astronaut. One an honours degree in engineering; two, a test pilot of ten years' experience; three, under 40. In the whole of America there were less than 100 men who qualified with these three conditions and about 70 of these were tested and the eventual first 7 astronauts selected from them. Of course they had to undergo fantastic trials and tests, but the one test that eliminated more candidates than any other single test was quite a simple one related to cold. They had to sit with both bare feet in a bucket of ice and water mush, where there is no danger of frostbite, but it is a test of extreme motivation. They had to do complex mental arithmetic at the same time.

I was not involved in selecting astronauts but involved in carrying out an experiment of a similar nature after one of our people had been and lived with Old Crow Indians in North America, who you would call Eskimos. Old Crow Indians never get frostbite.

They can take off their gloves when it is −20°C or −30°C and tie knots in their fishing line and put their gloves back on. If you tried to do this unless you had immediate help, not only would you not get your gloves back on but you would probably lose several fingers through frostbite.

Coming back to Britain, what he wanted to know was, is this inborn, is it ethnic, is it acquired or why does it happen to us and not to them? He looked for a group of people similar to Old Crow Indians and found them amongst people who fillet fish on the docksides where they stand in open sheds filleting fish all the year round and the fish, of course, were kept cooled in ice and water. When he tested them they behaved like Old Crow Indians. However, during the testing, one young man had just returned from National Service in the Army. Of course, he had not done any filleting of fish for two years and cried every day for two or three weeks until he got the acclimatisation back again.

The hands are very vulnerable because God did not know we were going to go out on the mountains when he gave us these beautiful five fingered hands, which have an enormous area to cool down. That is why we wear mitts instead of gloves when it is really cold.

COLD FEET

On a par with the hands and perhaps even more vulnerable are the feet and toes because they are more remote to us than our hands and they have a rather poor blood supply to them. It is very common talking to the older members of the Everest expeditions to find that they all lost an odd toe or two during their high Himalayan expeditions. They tell me the golden rule to remember is that if your feet feel cold do not worry about them. It is when they stop feeling cold, you worry because then they are beginning to freeze and you have no feeling in them.

ACCLIMATISATION

What the text books never seem to emphasise is acclimatisation to heat and cold. It is perhaps the most important aspect of all this physiology to realise that although we all have built within us the brain power to react to the heat and cold, nevertheless we can teach ourselves to react better in a process we call acclimatisation. In other words you have to go out in the cold to get used to being cold or go in the heat to get used to being hot.

Getting Hot

Getting used to the heat is comparatively easy because we all like to do it and it is a somewhat pleasurable process. We are all willing to go in saunas, or lie in hot baths. If you are going on holiday to a hot country and have access to a sauna, it is easy to get acclimatised to the heat, but even if you do not, if you just lie in a very hot bath for 20 minutes or half an hour every night for two weeks before you go, you will step out of the aeroplane and be pretty well acclimatised to the heat. You have learnt to do several things. One you sweat a bit earlier than you did before you were acclimatised so you do not get too hot before you start sweating and cooling down. Then you sweat and evaporate the sweat more efficiently and thirdly there are lots of other complex mechanisms within your body, one of which is that you increase the volume of the blood circulating within the body to cope with the extra blood you are going to push into the capillaries on your skin to lose heat. Along with acclimatisation which is an automatic process there is accustomisation. This is adapting to the heat in many ways – wearing suitable clothing, learning to drink more fluid, and then to slow down. If you have ever been to a tropical country you realise just how active people who live in Western Europe have become and unless you learn to slow down, you will have heat stress problems in the tropics. Unfortunately, alcohol is one of the worst things to drink in the tropics because along with almost every other drug it depresses the sweat rate and so for a given situation you will be hotter than you would if you had not had a drink of alcohol.

Getting Cold

It is quite possible for you to get acclimatised to cold but one finds, with experience, that people just do not like having cold showers or going out in the cold very much. I think we should be aware though that with modern civilisation we are largely losing our acclimatisation to cold. I am afraid my children are tired of hearing stories of my youth living in the North on the Derbyshire hills in a house which was only heated by one fire in the living room. In the winter one would awake just with the nose showing above the blankets and it was bright red from the cold. Then having to get out of bed and get dressed in a very cold bedroom. Also as a boy I had shorts inflicted upon me. We went to school with shorts and stockings and were just used to getting cold.

I remember going to the National Mountaineering Centre in North Wales soon after, at long last, they had acquired the money to fit central heating into all the bedrooms. The staff did somewhat regret the piece of luxury because they found in the winter it was much more difficult to go out with students on the hills than it had been when they were living a rather spartan life without central heating.

I often get asked if one should take people out on the hills in the winter when they have a tropical background? The answer is there is no scientific evidence shown that black or Asian people cannot stand the cold as well as any other ethnic group. In fact, one of the stories in all the text books of the lowest recorded deep body temperature of anyone who had recovered, is by a black woman who going home in the winter in Northern Canada, slipped, fell, banged her head and lay in very flimsy clothing all night in the street. In the morning she was taken to hospital and had a deep body temperature down to about 31 °C as far as I remember and recovered. If there is any problem with people from the West Indies, India or Africa, it is usually because their parents or even themselves have grown used to tropical climates and therefore have not had the training to choose the right clothing. It is not a physiological matter but more an ethnic and environmental problem.

FROSTBITE

Associated with the cold is this word frostbite, which just means that some part of the extremities usually fingers, thumbs or toes and ears and nose have been frozen solid. If parts of the anatomy have been frozen for any length of time then they are going to die and when they are thawed out will turn black, become gangrenous and will usually have to be amputated.

Fortunately for us frostbite is not very common in Britain because until the temperature reaches − 10°C the chances of frostbite are fairly small.

Associated with frostbite is the term "Trench-foot". This is a condition that was found amongst many soldiers in the First World War who for days, sometimes weeks, had been wearing boots and standing in mud or water which was not very cold but produced this effect of cold injury to the feet. A foot suffering from trench-foot is a grey colour and looks dead and may recover eventually but is often susceptible to cold for ever after.

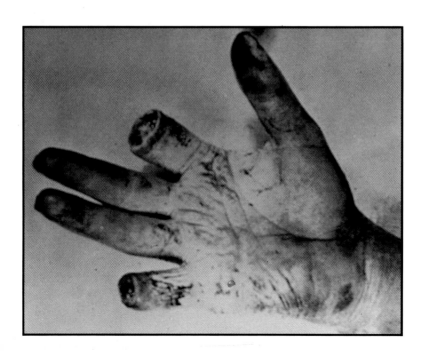

Knowing that fish filleters could get used to having their hands in ice and water we now tried experiments on our colleagues and friends at work. This environment at work was rather like having to sell raffle tickets where eventually having sold raffle tickets, inevitably you have to buy them from someone else. One had to persuade one's friends to be subjects in a small experiment (it was always a small experiment to start with), and eventually, of course, one would have to be subject to one of their experiments.

All we asked our subjects to do was to place their hand to about their wrist in a mush of ice and water which was contained in large open necked thermos flasks. We put a thermal couple to measure the temperature of the skin on one or two fingers and a thermal couple on the outside skin over the vein that passes over the elbow. They were quite warmly clad and merely had hands in ice and water. However, we had to stop the experiment because so many of our subjects who were just ordinary laboratory workers and scientists, fainted with the very painful effect produced by the ice and water mush. We found that the average time to faint was about three and a half minutes and this seemed to happen when the cold blood coming back to the body from the hand reached the chest wall.

This is just to illustrate how important cold can be long before it reaches dangerous levels.

HYPOTHERMIA AND EXPOSURE

As we have already said, hypothermia just means low temperature and this means the very dangerous condition that happens when the temperature of the deep body begins to drop and at a certain level everybody will die unless they receive very skilled medical attention. Just cooling the body to produce hypothermia will result in death if the cooling is severe enough and this could be accomplished in a laboratory quite easily. This is called acute hypothermia, which means that the cooling happened very quickly but death can occur from hypothermia when the cooling takes place over long periods of time, say, for example, when some old person lies in a cold flat without food or drink for several days, they will also die of hypothermia, but this is somewhat different.

When someone gets very cold on a mountain quite often medical opinion will say that they died from exposure. Exposure usually means that they have suffered from hypothermia which has been made much worse by the fact that they are also physically exhausted and have been battered about by the weather.

█ CLIMATE

Climate, or weather, whatever you want to call it, has such a major effect on the choice of equipment for expeditions that we should now just look at this major topic for a few moments.

If we imagine that we are planning an expedition, then obviously the climate of the part of the world we are going to would be the first matter to which we would give attention, that is we would know whether the area is desert, arctic, mountainous, jungle, or whatever. However, this is not in sufficient detail to help us plan the expedition fully as we do need to know very precise details of the area and even the sub area and finally the local conditions to which we will be taking the expedition.

It will be vital for you to know, therefore, very detailed accounts of the climate in the particular area you are going to visit. What will affect our bodily health and efficiency will be the conditions between the clothing between your body which we call MICRO CLIMATE. This is the conditions that you produce around your body by the clothing that you wear, which will, of course, be affected by the weather that is occurring outside the clothing.

In the tropics where light clothing will be worn, then perhaps the outside climate is the more important, but in areas of the world where a lot of clothing is worn, the micro climate becomes vital as this is the area that will affect the functioning of the body. For example, an eskimo although living in the conditions where there is severe cold, wears clothing which produces an almost tropical micro climate next to his skin. You would find that only his extremities are acclimatised to the cold because the rest of his body has been kept in a very warm condition by the wonderful clothing that he has evolved over generations.

Most of you will be taking part in expeditions in Great Britain, perhaps northern Europe, so let us look in some detail at the climate in Britain.

WIND AND WATER

Britain has a temperate climate but living in Britain we don't always appreciate how special our climate is. It has several features that are not found in the climate of other areas.

Being an island surrounded by water, and in the path of this stream of warm water, that we call the Gulf Stream, produces these rather special effects:

Ill-Defined Seasons. The four seasons in Britain tend to run into each other and the change from one to the other is not a definite time of the year, as I can remember, for example, having snow in May.

Sudden Changes in the Weather. These are a feature of the climate in Britain, hence the difficulty that the Meteorological Office has in providing weather forecasts further ahead than 24 hours.

Wet Climate. We don't appreciate, perhaps, that Britain is in an area where it gets considerable rainfall over the year.

Cold Rain. The rain in Britain, whenever it falls throughout the year, is always near O°C, so that we can have hailstones quite easily in the summer.

Rain any Day. In Britain we don't have particularly dry or particularly wet seasons, so it can rain on any day of the year.

Britain is rather a small island and the climate from one part of Britain to the other, is not very much different, whatever part of Britain you live in. So the clothes that people wear in Aberdeen are not very much different from those they wear in London. although I suppose the people in Aberdeen would have a heavier, thicker winter coat perhaps. However, if you do go up on the hills and are up to 1,000 feet or more, you would expect the climate to be a bit more severe.

Low temperature is not usually a problem in Britain as it is rarely below $-5°C$, even in Scotland, but nevertheless we get quite a lot of people who die from hypothermia or exposure on our hills. Most of these casualties occur not in the winter but in the summer, partly because there are more people on the hills in the summer than the winter. However, the main reason is that the two factors that cause the deaths from hypothermia and exposure in Britain are WIND AND WATER, hence the title of this section.

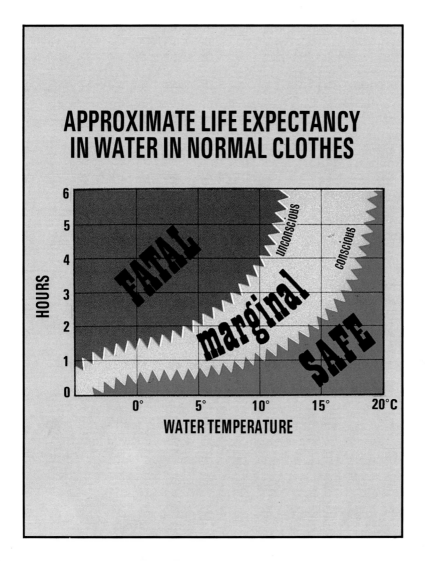

APPROXIMATE LIFE EXPECTANCY IN WATER IN NORMAL CLOTHES

EQUIVALENT CHILL TEMPERATURE CHART

AMBIENT TEMPERATURE (°C)

EQUIVALENT CHILL TEMPERATURE

WIND SPEED			4	2	0	-2	-4	-6	-8	-10	-12	-14	-16	-18	-20	-22	-24	-26	-28	-30	-32	-34	-36	-38	-40	-42	-44	-46	-48	-50
m/sec	KNOTS	MPH																												
4	8	9	-2	-4	-7	-9	-11	-14	-16	-19	-21	-23	-26	-28	-31	-33	-36	-38	-40	-43	-45	-48	-50	-52	-55	-57	-60	-62	-64	-67
6	12	13	-5	-8	-10	-13	-16	-18	-21	-24	-26	-29	-31	-34	-37	-39	-42	-44	-47	-50	-52	-55	-58	-60	-63	-66	-68	-71	-74	-76
8	16	18	-7	-10	-13	-16	-19	-21	-24	-27	-30	-33	-35	-38	-41	-44	-47	-49	-52	-55	-58	-61	-63	-66	-69	-72	-75	-77	-80	-83
10	19	22	-9	-12	-15	-18	-21	-24	-27	-30	-33	-35	-38	-41	-44	-47	-50	-53	-56	-59	-62	-65	-68	-70	-73	-76	-79	-82	-85	-88
12	23	27	-11	-14	-17	-20	-23	-26	-29	-32	-35	-38	-41	-44	-47	-50	-53	-56	-59	-62	-65	-68	-71	-74	-77	-80	-83	-86	-89	-92
14	27	31	-12	-15	-18	-21	-24	-27	-30	-33	-36	-39	-42	-45	-49	-52	-55	-58	-61	-64	-67	-70	-73	-76	-79	-82	-85	-89	-92	-95
16	31	36	-12	-16	-19	-22	-25	-28	-31	-34	-37	-41	-44	-47	-50	-53	-56	-59	-62	-66	-69	-72	-75	-78	-81	-84	-88	-91	-94	-97
18	35	40	-13	-16	-19	-22	-26	-29	-32	-35	-38	-41	-45	-48	-51	-54	-57	-61	-64	-67	-70	-73	-76	-80	-83	-86	-89	-92	-95	-99
20	39	45	-13	-17	-20	-23	-26	-29	-33	-36	-39	-42	-45	-48	-52	-55	-58	-61	-64	-68	-71	-74	-77	-80	-84	-87	-90	-93	-96	-100

WINDS ABOVE 20 m/sec HAVE LITTLE ADDITIONAL EFFECT

LITTLE DANGER   INCREASING DANGER   GREAT DANGER

Danger of freezing exposed flesh for properly clothed persons

[0

WATER

Water is going to be our major problem whenever we go out on expeditions in Britain. Water will come at us from two directions. First, the environment where it will come in the form of rain, sleet, snow or other wet items. Second, it will come from our body in the form of sweat and from an area we must not forget, from our breath which will become an important factor if we are looking at a tent with several people sleeping in it. Water is the factor that makes designing of equipment for Mount Everest or the South Pole easier than designing equipment for Britain, in that there is no water on Everest, only solid ice. Any equipment for Everest only has to be warm and wind-proof, it does not have to be waterproof.

Getting wet is a very serious problem and although we have all experienced the discomfort of condensation underneath a good waterproof outer, you should remember that you will never be as wet with sweat as you are with rain. Walking in the rain without a waterproof outer you will be absolutely saturated in a few minutes and being as wet as this has two factors which will produce serious consequences.

When clothing is saturated in water it no longer has any insulation, or virtually none, and all the advertisements that say that woollies are warm when wet are not founded on scientific fact. So, if your clothing is saturated in water, it is as though you are standing naked.

When the water evaporates it is going to remove heat from your body in order to evaporate and the amount of heat that it removes is considerable. If you take a cup of water, the amount of heat to evaporate the cup of water, is about five times the amount of heat to make that same cup boil.

If you do get soaked to the skin and you are somewhere in the hills or other outdoor environment, you must get to shelter immediately to remove the clothes and put on dry clothes if possible and, if this is not possible, the only solution for you is to get into a polythene bag when at least you stop the evaporation of the water and the effect of the wind.

WIND

The effects of wind on our body are equally dramatic to those of getting wet. You will see in the text an equivalent chill temperature chart which is a means of estimating the effect of wind on the rate at which it is going to cool your body. Let us take one example to show what happens. Say that if the air is at 0°C and you have a wind of 9 mph, then the effective temperature is − 4°C, the rate at which it is cooling you down is as though you were standing in air at − 4°C. As it is never still when you are out on the hills or out sailing, the effect of this wind chill is pretty evident. Perhaps you never go out in the winter, so let us take another example when if the air is 4°C, that is above freezing and there is a 9 mph wind, then the equivalent temperature is − 2°C, as though you were standing in air below freezing. I am sure we have all experienced this effect in many ways.

In some parts of the world, this wind chill effect is extremely serious, for example, in northern Canada in the winter when it may be − 20°C, which is very cold in terms of the winter in Britain, but in Canada people would be dressed for this sort of weather. However, if a wind blows up suddenly, children will not be released from school unless they are met by a parent with a vehicle because the effect of the wind will produce the cooling rate say as though it was − 30°C to − 35°C.

Thus, although Britain is a temperate climate and the winters are comparatively mild, there are still dangers from cooling down if we go out into the hills or go out sailing because of these two factors of getting wet and the wind chill effect.

A TRIP TO THE ARCTIC

Before leaving the topic of the climate in Britain, I must emphasise one of the problems that is so often forgotten. A Trip to the Arctic, is the title of the lecture I give to people who go sailing when I am discussing this topic with them.

I just want you to imagine that you are planning to lead an expedition to the Arctic and I know that you will never do this sort of journey to obtain your Gold Award with The Duke of Edinburgh's Scheme. But just bear with me for a few moments and the point of the exercise will become apparent. Before going to the Arctic, I am sure you know that you would spend many hours and many thousands of pounds making sure that you had the right clothing and equipment for the desperately cold temperatures that you would find and if you didn't have the right equipment then your lives would be in danger. Well I can tell you that many thousands of people, family sailors on yachts or in dinghies and so on who sail the seas around Britain are on "a Trip to the Arctic". If you are sailing around the coast of Britain, in winter or summer because the difference is quite academic, and you fall overboard then your life is in danger, not only from drowning but from cooling down so that you suffer from hypothermia. If you fall overboard off Clacton or Bournemouth, and I am talking about open sea and not in a shallow bay in Cornwall where the sand has warmed up the water, then when you are in the water you are going to lose heat from your body as though you were standing in those clothes, even if they are waterproofs, at the South or North Pole. That is how fast you are going to cool down and so your life is really on the line. That water in open seas around Britain rarely gets above 10°C or 12°C and can be as low as 2°C or 3°C. The lowest temperatures are not when you might expect them to be in the winter, but in the early spring when the Gulf Stream coming across the Atlantic from America shifts slightly northwards and this causes the very cold water, produced by melting glaciers in Norway, to be pushed down through the North Sea and the Channel. The temperature of the water can be as low as 2°C. Even in the summer when the temperature might be 12°C, your life can still be in danger, because the time it takes to cool down is not very different between the winter and the summer.

If you fall overboard then we must not forget that the quickest way to death is drowning and so you must have, no matter how good a swimmer you think you are, a good life-jacket if you are in deep water. A bouyancy aid is of value if you are a dinghy sailor in a reservoir and capsize and wish to swim back to the dinghy. You cannot swim in a proper life-jacket as a big proportion of the flotation is behind your head so that the life-jacket turns you on

your back. One of the major functions of a life-jacket is that you can lie on your back quite still in the water when you don't lose heat quite as fast as if you were trying to swim.

I am not going to give you a list of times showing if you fall into water at 5°C you have so many minutes, or if you fall into water at 10°C you have so many minutes, because it is not quite so precise as that. There are many people who are rescued from cold water who die on the way to hospital because they have reached the point of no return before they are rescued, although they are still alive. So, what we want to know is how long are you likely to have if you fall into cold water to give you a good chance of recovering if you get rescued and are taken to hospital.

From experiments that I have been involved with I can tell you that if you fall into water at 5°C, whether in just a swimming costume or ordinary clothing (it doesn't really make much difference) you are not going to be very happy after one hour, but if you are sensible and have on a wet suit then the time would be extended to about four hours. These times are only approximate and are for young, fit and healthy people, and not for middle-aged people who have heart trouble. I hope also that if you have the misfortune to fall overboard like this and are in the water for an hour, you will not look at your watch and say, right, I've had an hour and Don Robertson says that's the limit, and curl up and die, because survival is not like that. People have survived sometimes many hours in water at 5°C.

Equally at risk can be sail boarders who are not wearing wet suits and are continuously immersing themselves for short periods, or, dinghy sailors not wearing a wet suit who also can easily capsize several times. These people don't realise that they are building up, as it were, a cold debt and their body is slowly cooling which can reach dangerous limits if they are not careful.

I am not advocating that we stop sailing around the waters of Britain, but just that if you are going out into open sea be aware of the problems and take a few commonsense precautions. I would suggest the first item is a good lifeline so that you are clipped onto the boat and that you insist everybody has a good life-jacket and that they wear them. I am also amazed to find how many couples or families go out sailing and only dad is allowed to take the helm so that if dad has a heart attack and dies, which is not unknown, then nobody else has the faintest idea how to get the ship back to harbour. And how many wives or children have never taken the helm to practise man overboard, so that they are capable of bringing the boat around to search for a survivor, should this happen.

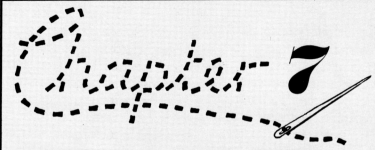

DEBUNKING THE MYTHS AND LEGENDS OF CLOTHING

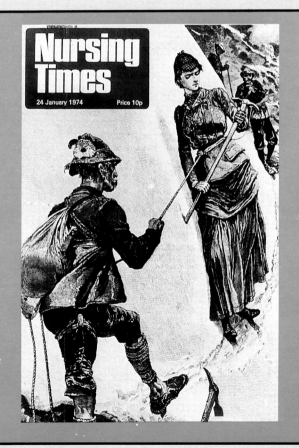

Nursing Times

24 January 1974   Price 10p

This chapter will undoubtedly be regarded by some people as an ego trip for an ageing expert in clothing. While accepting there is an element of truth in this statement, I would first like to say I hate to be called an expert. As an undergraduate at university we had a definition for the Professor which matches my definition of an expert. We thought, that as an undergraduate you enter university knowing a lot about a little and as you progress through the university to be a graduate and postgraduate, you learn more and more about less and less until as a Professor you know everything about nothing. That is what I regard an expert to be, someone who thinks he knows everything there is to know about his own topic and has shut his mind to learn anything else.

In this chapter I hope to explain some of the myths and legends and old wives' tales associated with clothing, because in no area of human activity is there such an abundance of old wives' tales etc as in clothing. Clothing in one form or another has been with us since man emerged from the trees. It is, therefore, not surprising that clothing has touched every aspect of human life from religion to food, sexual behaviour and so on. The very earliest garment in the form of a small apron was not worn for modesty or hygiene but probably on a religious magical level to stop the entry of dangerous magical spirits which may impair fertility. The proof of this is that even today amongst certain primitive tribes, the apron is worn at the front in men and over the buttocks in women. One of the most fascinating topics is the study of underwear or nether garments as they used to be called, because the original function of underwear was to keep your dirty body off the clean shirt or dress that you had just put on. Do not forget that then washing was a rather rare habit amongst everyone and the daily ritual of washing as we know it, is a very recent innovation. How the dictates of fashion have swung from one extreme to the other over the centuries.

Before we go on to discuss some of the legends associated with clothes, I would like to just put you in the picture and tell you a little of my background so that you will be able to make rational judgements about whether you believe my explanation of these myths and old wives' tales.

I graduated in Human Psychology and followed that with 5 years in textile research when modern fibres were just becoming commonplace. For the rest of the time I have been employed to carry out experiments using human subjects and designing specialised protective clothing for a large variety of different occupations. This chapter is heavily weighted by my scientific background as I have spent many years devising experiments in order to measure the various factors associated with wearing clothing. During all these experiences, I have always tried to measure as many factors as possible because, although it is important to ask the subjects opinion, it is not always a completely reliable guide to the quality of the clothing or equipment in use. Just as one example, I spent many hours of experimentation in helping to define "Thermal Comfort". This is, in simple words, the state which you spend most of your life where you are neither too hot nor too cold. If, for example, you are sitting at home watching television and you are beginning to get a bit cool, you either put on a jumper, sit nearer the fire or use some other technique quite unconscious of what you are doing and if you are too hot you do the opposite in order to stay in a cool situation. It is possible with modern scientific equipment to measure various factors on the human and you will know from these results whether he is thermally comfortable or whether he is too hot or too cold. We must keep ourselves in this state of thermal comfort, or perhaps, a better definition is thermal balance, because we must keep our body temperature, which really is the temperature of your blood, pretty constant and that is why the doctor, if you go and complain of feeling ill, always measures your temperature. A change in this temperature is a good indication of the sort of illness you have. We must keep our body temperature at 98°F or 37°C and no-one, no matter how strong, intelligent, tall, thin or fat, can tolerate his temperature rising very much above that without feeling very ill and eventually just dying. Equally if your body temperature drops by a degree centigrade then you are going to start feeling the effects and if your body temperature drops several degrees, then again, no matter how tough or strong you are, you will die. These two conditions are known in medical terms as hyper-thermia, or fever is a more common name for a raised body temperature and hypo-thermia for a body temperature that is below normal.

So my opinions are going to be very much swayed by a scientific background but they are tempered, I hope, by the experiences of early childhood where I grew up in a small village in the North of England living a very rural semi-farming existence on the Cheshire side of the Derbyshire hills. I am afraid I was considered something of a "sissy" by many of the local people because I took an interest in anything that was artistic and scientific so just wandered about collecting flowers and butterflies and various other things.

PHYSIOLOGY OF CLOTHING

Many thousands of people work in the clothing business designing and making up clothes which are largely worn for their fashion and artistic appeal. On the other hand, very few people in the world work on the function of clothing and how it affects our body and so on. Some people work designing clothing for protection in factories but it is largely done on an historical basis and not as a result of experiments. It is quite difficult to work with people on experiments in the choice of different items of clothing. For example if we were comparing shirt (a) and shirt (b), it is very difficult to design an experiment where the subject does not know that he is wearing shirt (a) or (b) but to carry out any scientific experiment people must not know which item they are wearing.

Thermal Comfort

We must just return for a few moments to this idea of thermal comfort as much of the discussion to follow will include references to this state of our body. We spend much of our life with our deep body, that is really the temperature of our blood at or near 37°C, that is 97°F.

But the temperature of your skin, as I am sure you are aware, can vary quite considerably, so that the skin on your hands and feet can be quite cool, while the skin on your belly and back will be quite warm. However, if you measured the temperature of the skin all over your body and made an average, you would find it

would be 90°F/33°C. You would find differences amongst
people, especially between men and women where the skin
temperature of women's legs wearing a skirt and nylon stockings
would be lower than the temperature of men's legs wearing thick
trousers. But nevertheless the average would still be 90°F or
33°C and we make most of our judgements about comfort on this
average skin temperature not on a change in our deeper body
temperature and we control this skin temperature by opening or
shutting the tiny blood vessels of which there are many thousands
in our skin and surface layers. Man has learnt to control these
temperatures very accurately by changing clothing or by the use
of artificial heating, like fires.

Sweating

We are always losing small amounts of liquid from our body
because our skin is not completely waterproof but this is not true
sweating. Sweating is an active process where we have millions of
tiny glands opening onto our skin which produce a salty liquid
that we call sweat. This is a means of keeping cool whereby the
sweat evaporates off our skin and takes heat with it. We start
sweating when our brain senses that the temperature on our skin
on average has reached 95°F or 35°C. Man is a tropical animal
and is much better at keeping cool than keeping warm. We can
produce an enormous amount of sweat if we get really hot. The
danger is, of course, by sweating you are taking water from your
body and if this is not replaced you begin to dehydrate and your
brain has a means of sensing this, so that we begin to reduce the
amount of sweat we are producing and therefore get hotter. Also
we have means whereby we can become acclimatised to a heat
which just means that our body is a bit more efficient at sweating,
that is all. So if you are going on holiday to a hot country,
acclimatise yourself to the heat by lying for half an hour or so in a
very very hot bath each night for two weeks before you go and
then when you are there each morning before you go out drink
several glasses of water or orange juice to replace the liquid you
are going to lose by sweating during the day.

Shivering

We respond to a small amount of cold by cutting down the blood going to our skin and this we use all the time and is very effective. If, however, the cooling process continues we have means of producing heat by shivering, which just means that your brain tells all your muscles to move and so generate heat without moving the limbs to which the muscles are attached. It is possible to produce large amounts of heat by shivering but it is a very tiring process. If you carry on cooling down in spite of shivering then eventually you will go unconscious and die because your body temperature will reach a critical figure. So shivering is a good flag to look for and if you have been shivering or you see someone else has been shivering for more than half a minute or so, beware and do something to stop it by putting on more clothes, getting dry or anything to get yourself warm again.

Cold-Water Immersion

Nowhere in the world can you lie in the sea and not cool down,
except of course in a shallow bay somewhere or other, but in
the open sea the water is always cooling you down. Swimming
just makes you cool quicker and one of the major functions of a
good life-jacket is that you can lie still in the water and therefore
not cool down so fast. Most people do not realise how very
dangerous it is to fall in the sea wearing ordinary clothing, that is
to say a set of waterproofs, and it does not matter whether it is
winter or summer, your life is going to be in danger from hypothermia. If you fall into the sea off the coast of Britain whether it is
winter or summer even if you are young, fit and healthy, your life
is going to be in danger very quickly and you will certainly be
very lucky to survive a few hours immersed in the sea. My lecture
to the sailing fraternity I entitle "A Trip to the Arctic". This is to
bring home the problem of falling into the sea because if you fall
in the sea off Clacton in the summer wearing a set of waterproof
trousers and jacket you will be losing heat as though you were
standing in those clothes at the North Pole. And of course if you
were going to the North Pole, you would take precautions and
wear special clothing but people sail in the sea off Clacton and do
not think about the danger of cooling down if they fall overboard.

Human Fat

Unfortunately the modern fashion of very thin people has made
us more vulnerable to the cold as a layer of fat is a very good
insulator. Just picture an African native and an Eskimo and I am
sure you will all be thinking of a tall thin slender African and a
small round cherubic-looking Eskimo. The difference of course is
in the amount of body fat and you would find that all the people
who are cross-channel swimmers are much more like Eskimos
than the thin African, although the Olympic swimmer would
probably resemble the slender African. During a series of famous
experiments in the '50s two kinds of swimmer were used, one
famous Olympic swimmer and a famous cross-channel swimmer

were put into baths where the water had been cooled to about 5°C
or 10°C. They were told to swim as hard as they could to try and
keep warm and the cross-channel swimmer could swim more or
less for ever but the olympic swimmer had to be pulled out of the
water in about 30 odd minutes because he was in danger of going
unconscious due to the cold. When they put a good wet suit on
the Olympic swimmer behaved very much like the cross-channel
swimmer and the wet suit kept him warm.

Getting Cold

We hope that none of you will ever be in the position where the
cold is so intense that you are going to die from hypothermia but
if you go outdoors whether walking, sailing, canoeing or
mountaineering, then you will experience getting cold much more
than if you were staying at home watching television. The first
thing to remember is that when you get cold you get very stiff and
you would find it very difficult to open a button, strike a match or
if you are in an emergency, let off a flare or other rescue device.
Also getting cold is very distracting and has a marked effect on
our concentration and other faculties of the brain.

Manmade Fibres

In my travels I meet many people who say "Oh I couldn't wear
anything made from man made fibres" and so on and I hate to
disillusion them, but it is very difficult, unless you are a millionaire,
to buy any garment that is 100% natural fibres. All the clothes we
wear in this day and age have a contribution from manmade
fibres, if only the sewing threads or the inter-linings or some
similar item. Even if the fabrics themselves are made from 100%
natural fibres the fabric is often treated in order to give it some
particular quality like, for example, washability in a washing
machine. I can guarantee that if you were the subject in a highly
technical scientific experiment in clothing, where you would be
blindfolded and dressed in garments worn next to your skin made
from a whole range of different fibres, including natural and
manmade fibres, you would find it impossible to tell what fibre
any garment was made of.

The old wives' tales of nylon being very hot and sweaty are the results of people buying the only wonder fabric available at the end of the Second World War and that was parachute nylon. This fabric was sold in large quantities to ladies who made underwear and nightdresses from it as it had this lovely diaphanous silky feel about it. However, having been finished for parachutes it had a very low air porosity and therefore a very low transmission of water vapour and wearing a nightdress made from parachute nylon is rather like sleeping in a polythene bag, although the nylon is very thin. It is now possible to texture weave knit and finish manmade fibres so that they have enormous appeal to our various senses like touch, feel and colour.

We have, of course, discovered that adding a manmade fibre to a natural fibre produces a much better fabric in many ways. For example, men's suits made from mixtures of terylene and wool are much better to wear than the traditional pure wool fabrics. Although we do appreciate the qualities of cotton, a blouse or skirt made from pure cotton fibres is very difficult to iron, wash and so on. So we have gone to the extent of making "core spun yarns", which means that we take a filament of terylene or nylon or other manmade fibre and wrap round it a thread of cotton so we combine the best of both worlds. We have the cotton next to us but the core of manmade fibre gives us very good crease resistance and easy wash/wear properties.

In any event there is just not enough silk in the world to clothe everybody in silk. Our beliefs, in so many facets of modern life, are in social acceptance, for example as a boy one would never admit that you had to take hire purchase to buy a bicycle or some other item, it was just not socially acceptable to be in debt. But now everybody without exception has some sort of hire purchase, loan agreement, bank loan or whatever. I have seen the same happen in knitted garments, where originally everybody would pretend and in fact declare openly that all their pullovers or jumpers were 100% pure wool and would not like to admit that they had been bought an acrylic jumper. Now if one looks through shops, whether expensive or cheap shops, you will find a whole range of garments from pure wool to pure acrylic and what we have got used to, which was just not present a few years ago, are the beautiful colours and patterns of modern knitted garments.

Advertising

I think we must accept that we cannot totally believe any
advertisements that we read in the newspaper or on a hoarding or
wherever. The best firms do not tell lies but they do not tell us all
the truth. Thinking of the outdoors we do get many articles in lots
of the magazines where they review sleeping bags, waterproofs or
what have you, but we must remember that the bulk of the
income for the magazine is not in the price that you pay for it, but
in the revenue from advertising. No magazine is going to carry
articles which condemn items of equipment that are advertised in
another part of a magazine.

Expeditions

We are always being bombarded with statements that Mr X, the
famous mountaineer, had worn the jacket in the Himalayas or
other wild place in the world and said it was the finest jacket he
had ever worn. Just put yourself in the place of Mr X for a few
moments. You are planning a trip to some wild place in the world
which is going to cost you thousands of pounds and you are
always short of money. Then out of the blue comes a letter from a
clothing firm saying they have made this jacket for you, and all
they want you to do is wear it in the wild place you are going to
and try it for them and write a report when you come home. Now
is any sensible expeditioner going to wear the jacket and come
home and say it is the worst jacket he has ever worn? Especially
when the firm have said they will give him £5,000 towards the
expedition. He knows unless he comes home and says it is the most
wonderful jacket, the next time he goes abroad he is not going to
get this sponsorship from any firm.

Even if our expeditioner has genuinely worn the jacket in the
wild places, which is not always the case, and even if he is
genuinely interested in testing equipment, let us face it that the
expedition is going to consume most of his energy and be the
priority in his thoughts. If for example he is trying to climb
Everest it is like running a marathon with a 200 lb weight pack on
his back and nobody under these circumstances is going to have
the time or the inclination to do real trials and tests on any piece
of equipment when his main object is to get to the top of the
mountain. It is sad to see famous people come home and give

quotations which are repeated in advertisements saying that this particular garment is, for example, "warm when wet". In the 1950s there were some famous experiments carried out by Dr Pugh, who was physiologist with Lord Hunt on his successful Everest expedition, when he carried out scientific experiments as the result of the death of a hill walker taking part in one of those hill walking races. The man died as a result of hypothermia and exposure after walking all day in rain and Dr Pugh showed that he had been wearing a T-shirt and shorts and measured the insulation value of the clothing when it was wet. His results showed us for the first time what water does on the insulation value of clothing, as he measured the insulation of the clothing when dry and then when wet with rain and the insulation value then was one tenth of the value when the clothes were dry.

Textile Testing

Unfortunately 90% of all textile testing is done on small pieces of
fabric in the laboratory. This is an inevitable consequence of the
time and cost of trying to carry our experiments under real
conditions, especially if you are using human subjects for these
experiments. Picture yourself as a clothing manufacturer having
20 or 30 different fabrics to choose from. You would not have the
time or the money or even the inclination to make all these
different fabrics into garments to try them outdoors. So the
industry has developed a whole series of laboratory tests which
imitate the various factors that clothing will meet when they are
worn by people or put onto settees or car seats or whatever.

Human Trials

What we would really like to see is systematic testing of equipment
and clothing on people. We would ask their opinion, but we
would also try and measure as many factors as we could. I know
of no firm which manufactures clothing and equipment for
outdoors which has a facility to carry out such trials. There have
been extensive trials of this sort but almost entirely carried out by
Government agencies for armed forces or similar people and it is a
great shame that the results of these trials are not made available
to the general public.

Let us just look at a few of the factors that are tested routinely by
textile manufacturers.

Space Blankets

A so-called "Space-Blanket" is sold by shops as an item of Survival
Equipment. It is comparatively expensive (£2–£3 in 1988) but
much favoured by people because it is a very small packet –
6cm × 6cm × 3cm. It consists of a sheet of aluminium plastic, not
aluminium foil, which you may know unaluminised as "Cook-
bags". It is in fact Mylar or a similar material.

In case of emergency when someone is getting hypothermia you
are told to unfold this sheet of very thin plastic and wrap it
around the "body". The silver blanket is supposed to keep you
warm, although it is very thin by reflecting your body heat.

The same principle is used in the capes presented to people as they complete the London Marathon. There are even articles in the medical journal *Lancet* 1968; Vol. 1, page 672, reported by the *New Scientist* in April 1968; where babies are kept warm by wrapping them in this silver blanket.

I am sorry to say that they have all been victims of a blatant use of advertising to give the impression of a high tech product from "SPACE".

The aluminising has very little effect in keeping you warm – you would be as warm wrapped in thin polythene.

We must look for a moment at the physics of heat to understand the problem.

Heat passes from one object to another by four ways:
Convection
Conduction
Radiation
Evaporation in man

Convection is the shimmer we see over a fire as heat rises and the air is warmed.

Conduction is the contact with another body. Lying on cold ground is an obvious case hence the reason for a mat to sleep on.

Radiation is where heat travels in rays, like light, but in rays that we cannot see called INFRA RED. You feel these rays when you warm your hands in front of a fire.

Now imagine you are lying injured on the hills. You are losing heat by Convection and an enormous amount of heat by "FORCED CONVECTION" when the wind blows over you (also by evaporation if you are wet).

You will be losing heat by Conduction if you are lying on the cold earth (hence a foam mat underneath is essential).

You will be losing very little heat by Radiation because you are not a very "hot" body. The amount of heat loss by radiation between two articles depends on the difference in temperature between the two articles, but until this difference is about 100°C not much heat is passed. When you warm your hands, the fire you are using is 500°C.

Infra Red rays although very similar to light rays, will not pass through some materials that light will pass through easily. For example, infra-red rays will not pass through glass – get an electric bar fire, feel the heat, then put a sheet of glass between you and the fire – no heat.

If the authors of the articles about Space Blankets had tried using the clear plastic instead of aluminised plastic they would have been just as warm.

To prove or disprove this statement we set up experiments in a cold chamber. If you wish to read the full Report it is published in Aviation, Space and Environmental Medicine January 1977.

We chose three climates, all giving the same rate of cooling.

First to imitate a snow hole
Still air at −25°C.

Second, Winter in Northern Europe.
Wind 12 mph −8°C.

Third, Winter in Great Britain.
High Wind 0°C.

The subjects wore clothing more suited to the English summer than winter. However, we did wrap up the face and neck to stop frostbite. A scarf sealed the neck and stopped air getting in the bag. Subjects lay on a foam mat. Although we were interested in the opinion of subjects the main results came from measuring their heat loss. The plastic sheets were made into a man-sized bag for convenience and better reproducibility of results.

Four different bags were used:
Polythene sheet 12 mm thick.
Clear Melinex sheet 17 microns thick.
Aluminised Melinex Aluminised side out.
Aluminised Melinex Aluminised side in.

Results

There was no significant difference in the cooling between any of the bags!! So a polythene bag was as good as any other.

We used bags because sheets of material were unmanageable in any sort of wind. Wrapping people in a sheet of plastic is not a practicable process in the outdoors.

We could not use the conditions at 0°C as the three Melinex bags were all torn to shreds in a few minutes by the flapping of the material in the wind. The polythene bag would stand winds up to 40 mph and still not tear.

These results have serious implications for "Space Blankets" in survival. First, a sheet is useless and the aluminised sheet will tear to shreds in wind. The laboratory results have been borne out by trials on the hills. The Melinex is extremely strong for its thickness and you cannot push a finger through the Melinex. Once you have a pin-hole in the Melinex, it just tears instantly. The polythene will allow a finger to poke through but is more "rubbery" than Melinex so will not tear easily even when holed.

We found on the hills that when a subject lay down in the heather, the Melinex was soon punctured and the bag of Melinex lasted all of 10 minutes. A thin polythene bag lasted the whole of the trial – about 5 days.

Why "Space Blanket"?

On the moon, an astronaut encounters extremes of temperature. Standing on the moon the astronaut is losing or gaining heat, how? – No convection as there is no air, little conduction as only his feet are in contact – so Radiation – heat from infra red is a very big portion of the heat transfer.

What the advertisements do not tell you are that you have one layer of aluminised plastic, where an astronaut has fifty layers of the material separated by forty-nine layers of a very thin tissue-paper like material.

If you have a Space Blanket I will give you a prize if you can tell me which side is aluminised. Only one side is aluminised and you can tell with a simple battery, bulb circuit. The aluminised side conducts electricity and the other side (Melinex) does not.

The aluminised side does reflect infra-red the other side absorbs infra-red.

Which side (if you knew) would you ideally put towards you? I will leave you to confront your Physics teacher for the answer.

The instructions with a Space Blanket also claim that it is very useful in Survival as a Radar Reflector – this we have also found to be untrue.

Now you are going to think I am a hypocrite when I tell you that I am going to recommend that in some survival kits you should put a sheet of aluminised plastic – for what? Well in the brilliant sun of the desert a sheet of this mirror-like plastic reflects the sun and casts a very cool shadow.

Sunshine

Before leaving this topic I hope you will be willing to read just a little more physics. Sunshine is a very special item. We have already said that infra-red rays (the heat) will not pass through glass. How then do you get very hot behind the glass window of a coach in the sun? How does a green-house get so hot?

Sunshine is remarkable in that the bulk of the heat from the sun is in the visible light not the infra-red. In a green-house the sun streams through the glass – the heat warms the soil and the plants, but they send out the heat as infra-red. These rays cannot pass through the glass so the heat from the sunshine stays in the green-house.

Different colours reflect infra-red rays differently – polished metals, silver best and then aluminium – reflect 95% of infra-red. Black absorbs the rays but by checking the roofs of cars on a hot sunny, still day you will find only white reflects well – pale blue or red reflect like black.

In the desert the temperature can reach 50°C in the shade but the dark rocks will be 100°C.

Polythene Bags

A polythene bag can save your life on the hills in an emergency.
I suggest you may take two bags – a thick orange one in the
rucksac and the very thin (120 gauge) in your pocket. Polythene
tubing can be bought at many Garden Centres where the 120
gauge will be about 20–30p per metre (1988) 75 cm wide.

COATED FABRICS

	Base fabric	Coating	Weight Gms/sq m.	Uses
1.	Nylon plain	Polyurethane PU	80	Tent fly, lightweight waterproofs
2.	Nylon plain	PU	150	Anoraks, trousers, stuffsacks, groundsheets
3.	Nylon ripstop	PU	70–150	Tent flysheets, light-weight waterproof clothing
4.	Nylon plain	PU	240	Heavy-duty waterproofs Gaiters, rucksacs, panniers
5.	Textured nylon	PU	375	CORDURA Nylon looks like canvas. Very heavy-duty. Rucksacs, gaiters, only patches on clothes.
6.	Nylon plain	ACRYLIC		Cheap coating. Bad for cracking
7.	Nylon ripstop	Silicone elastomer	65–80	New proofing, very strong. Flysheets for tents. Bivi bags.
8.	Nylon plain	Neoprene	180–190	Lightweight Anorak, trousers, mitt outers, Bumbags.
9.	Nylon plain	Neoprene	240	Heavy-duty waterproof jacket and trousers, gaiters, rucksacs.
10.	Knitted nylon	PU transfer coated		Leather-look, soft to wear
11.	All cotton	Wax		The country-look – for you.

NON-COATED FABRICS

	Base Fabrics	Weight	Uses
(a)	Plain nylon	80–150	Linings
(b)	Ripstop nylon	50–75	Glazed surface to reduce air porosity. Downproof.
(c)	Anti-Gliss Polyester nylon Cotton	150	Non-slip surface for skiing. Downproof. Can have water-repellent finish. Scotchguard.
(d)	Canvas Cotton	140–230	Tight-woven for tent outers. Traditionally proofed.
(e)	Fibre pile Knitted back Nylon back Acrylic and Polyester pile	Various weights	Imitation 'fur'. Often has anti-pill on back. For jackets, sleeping-bags – non-polished pile.
(f)	Fibre pile Laminated backing	Various	Pile fabrics with another fabric as face – reduce wind penetration.
(g)	Fleece Polyester		Brushed fabrics (like blankets). Can be brushed on both sides.
(h)	Super fleece		Two layers of fleece bonded together.
(i)	Ventile 100% cotton	180–250	Very special light woven cotton. Very windproof. Jackets, Tents etc. Water repellent finish.

BREATHABLE FABRICS

Used in UK
Polyurethane Coatings
Courtaulds
Aquation 3
Carringtons
Cyclone
Finlayson
Action 500

PTFE film laminates
Gordon and Fairclough
Ability
Gore Corporation
Goretex

Cotton Ventiles
Thomas Mason Ltd.

Cotton Ventile L28
Cotton Ventile L34
Cotton Ventile L24
Cotton Ventile L19

TRADE NAMES OF MAN-MADE FIBRES

Regenerated Cellulose

1. Cellulose Acetate

Cela Fibre (staple)	British Celanese Ltd
Dicel (continuous filament)	Ditto
Lansil	Lansil Ltd

Acetate fabrics have a soft handle and good draping qualities. They also dye easily and are quick drying. Acetate is therefore used in lingerie dresses and sportswear. Most coat linings are Acetate.

2. Cellulose Triacetate

Arnel	Celanese Fibers, U.S.A.
Tricel	British Celanese

Triacetate fabrics are similar to Acetate fabrics but have lower moisture absorption and higher softening temperatures. They are therefore used for fashion designs for permanent pleating.

3. Rayon

(**a**) Cuprammonium rayon

Bemberg	Bemberg, West Germany
Cupressa	Bayer, West Germany

Cuprammonium rayon is very "silk" like and is used for underwear and linings

(**b**) Viscose rayon

Courtaulds rayon	Courtaulds Ltd
Fibro	Ditto

Viscose rayon is about the cheapest fibre made. Poor wet strength but very absorbent.

(**c**) Modified rayon

Durafil (high tenacity)	Courtaulds Ltd
Evlan (coarse, crimped)	Ditto
Sarille (fine crimped)	Ditto
Tenasco (high tenacity)	Ditto
Vincel (polynosic)	Ditto

High tenacity rayon is used where strength is needed e.g. tyre cords, tapes, sewing threads, etc.
Crimped fibres are found in carpets etc.

Synthetic Fibres

Acrylic

Acrilan	Monsanto Ltd
Courtelle	Courtaulds
Orlon	Du Pont

Acrylic fibres are very wool like but much cheaper. They are used extensively in cheap knitwear and mixed with wool in more expensive garments.

Modacrylic

Dynel	Union Carbide Ltd
Teklan	Courtaulds

Modacrylic fibres are made to be less flammable than normal acrylics.

Chloro-Fibres

Rhovyl (P.V.C.)	Soc Rhyvyl France
Saran	BX Plastics

These fibres are non-absorbent. The best known example is Damart underwear.

Glass Fibres

Glass fibres are not used in garments. Best known for insulating lofts etc and in making boats, helmets etc with resin.

Metallic Fibres

Lurex	Dow Chemicals

Glittery Lurex is known to everybody in all kinds of clothing.

Polyamide (Nylon)

(**a**) Nylon 6

Enkalon	British Enkalon
Perlon	Germany

(**b**) Nylon 6.6

Antron (trilobal)	Du Pont
Bri Nylon	I.C.I.
Blue C Nylon	Monsanto
Cantree (Bicomponent)	Du Pont
Du Pont Nylon	

Nylon is the most used of all man-made fibres. Cheap, very strong, easily dyed, and so it is found in use from ropes to nylon stockings.

Polyester

Dacron	Du Pont
Terlenka	British Enkalon
Terylene	I.C.I.
Trevira	Heochst

Polyester fibres are very strong and also make beautiful fabrics. They would have a wider application but for the cost. They have a wide use in mixtures with wool for suitings.

Polyethelene (Polythene)

Courlene	British Celanese
Drylene	
Ulstron	I.C.I.
Meraklon (Polypropylene)	S.p.a. Italy

These fibres are completely non-absorbent but have extensive use in thermal underwear. As the fibres float they make good nets. Used in carpet backing threads for carpets because they are so cheap.

Polyurethane

Lycra	Du Pont
Spanzelle	Courtaulds

Polyurethane fibres are just like elastic. They produce stretch fabrics for swimwear, tights etc.

Textured Yarns

Textured yarns are made from nylon and terylene yarns.

Agilon	Nylon
Banlon	Nylon
Courtolon	Nylon
Crimplene	Terylene
Fluflene	Terylene
Fluflon	Nylon
Helenca	Nylon and Terylene
Lancola	Acetate
Taslan	Air jet textured system

Texturing yarns add various properties to simple yarns.
Helenca stretch fabrics.

There are over 1000 different fibres marketed in the world that are
chemically different, and each one will be made in several different
deniers etc, the variations must be counted in several thousands.

ENERGY REQUIREMENTS

Activity	CAL/m²/HR	CALS/MAN/HR
Sleeping	36	64.8
Sleeping/digesting	40	72
Lying quietly	40	72
Lying and digesting	46	82.8
Sitting	50	90
Standing	60	108
Stroll $1\frac{1}{2}$ mph	90	162
Level walk 3 mph	130	234
Level walk 4 mph	180	324
Level run 10 mph	500	900
Sprinting	2,000?	
Walk 5% grad. $3\frac{1}{2}$ mph	220	396
Walk 10% grad. $3\frac{1}{2}$ mph	340	612
Work exhausting (Young man)	over 380	684

WORK RATES AND WATER EVAPORATION FROM THE SKIN

Work Rate in Watts	Equivalent Water Evaporation Rate from the skin gms/water/24 hours
15	570
100	3800
200	7600
300	11500
400	15200
500	19000

After Keighley.

CONVERSION FACTORS

Degrees Fahrenheit °F	Degrees Celsius °C

°F   Subtract 32
Multiply by 5 divide by 9

−40°F	= −40°C
32°F	= 0°C
212°F	= 100°C
98.6°F	= 37°C

Degrees Celsius °C	Degrees Fahrenheit °F

°C   Multiply by 9 divide by 5
Then add on 32

−40°C	= −40°F
0°C	= 32°F
100°C	= 212°F

CONVERSION FACTORS

Multiply the Number of	BY	To obtain the Equivalent of
Inches (in)	2.54	Centimetres (cm)
Yards (yd)	0.91	Metres (m)
Centimetres (cm)	0.39	Inches (in)
Metres (m)	1.09	Yards (yd)
Square Yards (sq yd)	0.84	Square Metres (sq m)
Square Metres (sq m)	1.2	Square Yards (sq yd)
Ounces (oz)	28.3	Grams (gms)
Grams (gms)	0.035	Ounces (oz)
Ounces/Yard	34.2	Grams/Metre
Grams/Metre	0.029	Ounces/Yard

AVERAGE SIZES

Men
Anorak – Jacket

Sizes	Chest	Garment size Chest	B—B on Pattern I	Garment Length C—C on Pattern		
				Norm	$\frac{3}{4}$	Full
Small	34	45	$22\frac{1}{2}$	30	35	39
Small	36	48	24	30	35	40
Medium	38	50	25	31	36	41
Medium	40	52	26	31	36	41
Large	42	54	27	32	37	42
Large	44	56	28	32	37	42
X-Large	46	58	29	33	38	43

Women
Anorak – Jacket

Sizes		Chest Bust	Garment sizes Bust	B—B on Pattern I
Small	10	33	43	$21\frac{1}{2}$
Medium	12	34	44	22
Medium	14	36	46	23
Large	16	38	48	24
Large	18	40	50	25
X-Large	20	42	52	26

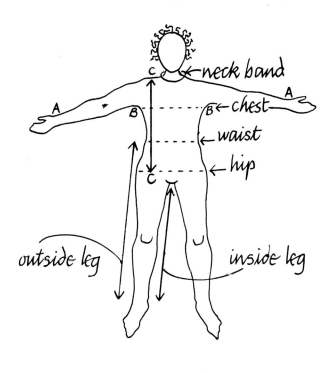

Body measurements
see text

neck band

chest

waist

hip

outside leg

inside leg

FIG. 46

UNIVERSAL CLOTHING SIZES

Men's Suits

UK/USA (in)	34	35	36	37	38	39	40	41	42	43	44	45	46	47	48
UK (cm)	86		91		97		102		107		112		117		122

Men's Hats

UK	6⅝	6¾	6⅞	7	7⅛	7¼	7⅜	7½	7⅝	7¾
USA	6¾	6⅞	7	7⅛	7¼	7⅜	7½	7⅝	7¾	7⅞
EEC	54	55	56	57	58	59	60	61	62	63

Men's Footwear

UK	5	5½	6	6½	7	7½	8	8½	9	9½	10	10½	11	11½	12
USA	5½	6	6½	7	7½	8	8½	9	9½	10	10½	11	11½	12	12½
EEC	38½	39	39½	40	41	41½	42	42½	43	44	45	45½	46	46½	47

Women's Clothes

UK (sizes)	8	10	12	14	16	18	20
Bust/Hip (in)	31/33	32/34	34/36	36/38	38/40	40/42	42/44
Bust/Hip (cm)	80/85	84/89	88/93	92/97	97/102	102/107	107/112

USA (sizes)	8	10	12	14	16	18	20
Bust/Hip (in)	32/34	33/35	34½/36½	36/38	37½/39½	39/41	41/43

GERMANY (sizes)	34	36	38	40	42	44	46
Bust/Hip (cm)	80/86	84/90	88/94	92/98	96/102	100/106	104/110

SPAIN/PORTUGAL (sizes)	36	38	40	42	44	46	48
Bust/Hip (cm)	78/84	82/88	86/92	90/96	94/100	98/104	104/110

FRANCE (sizes)	34	36	38	40	42	44	46
Bust/Hip (cm)	81/89	84/92	87/95	90/98	93/101	96/104	102/110

ITALY (sizes)	38	40	42	44	46	48	50
Bust/Hip (cm)	82/84	85/88	88/92	91/95	94/100	97/104	100/108

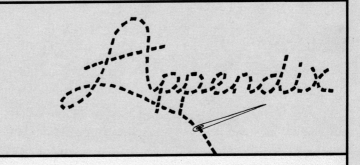

SUPPLIERS

Many fabrics can be bought at a good fabric shop and if you are lucky enough to have a market, many bargains can be bought.

The problem fabrics are the proofed ones. As I have never seen these fabrics in shops, I have given a list of suppliers.

The sundries – i.e. buckles, eyelets, webbing, etc, can now be bought at most Camping, Outdoor shops.

It may be that you have a textile manufacturer near (or your sister, cousin or aunt has). Make friends with them as there are some excellent bargains to be had if you go along and pay cash!

Paper for patterns can usually be obtained, free of charge, from printers as they are often glad to get rid of ends of rolls.

If you require small amounts of the fabrics below I can supply them. Or if you wish to purchase a roll (100 metres) or half a roll, discount can be arranged.

$2 + 2 - 4oz/yd =$	135gm/sq m	Neoprene coated nylon.
$4 + 4 - 8oz/yd =$	270gm/sq m	Neoprene coated nylon.
2 oz	= 68gm/sq m	Ripstop Silicone Elastomer proofed
2 oz	= 68gm/sq m	Plain weave PU proofed.
2 oz	= 68gm/sq m	Plain weave nylon unproofed.
4 oz	= 135gm/sq m	Nylon PU proofed.
2 oz	= 68gm/sq m	Ripstop unproofed Ventile as available.

D. G. Robertson
8 The Woodlands
Brightlingsea
Colchester
Essex CO7 ORY
Telephone Brightlingsea 2777.

Names and Addresses

Hamish Hamilton
Unit 14
Meersbrook Mill
Valley Road
Sheffield s89 4BI

Point North Ltd.
Box DGR
58 High Street
Cemaes Bay
Anglesey
Gwynedd LL67 0HL
Telephone (0407) 711030

Pennine Outdoor
Box DGR
Hard Knott
Holmbridge
Huddersfield
West Yorkshire HD7 1NT
Telephone (0484) 684302

Thomas Mason Ltd
Primet Hill
Colne
Lancs BB8 8DP
Telephone (0282) 863535

Scout Shops
Churchill Industrial Estate
Lancing
Sussex BN15 8UG
Telephone (0903) 755352

John Burgess
24 Creswell Avenue
Staplegrove
Taunton
Somerset TA2 6LR

Service

Manufacturers Buffalo Sleeping
Bags – Fibre Pile. Sells Fibre
Pile fabric. Very good service.
Interested in helping.

Large postal trade. All fabrics at
retail prices. Interested in
helping. Retail Ventile.

Large postal trade. All fabrics at
retail prices. Interested in
helping.

Ventile manufacturer. Ask for
Mr S. West or Mr D. Wilson.

Large chain of retail shops –
profit back to Scouts. Stockists
of D of E Scheme Anoraks,
Rucksacs, Tents, etc.
Ask for Martin Penstone.

A one-man firm who is a
specialist in rucksacs. He will
supply anything to do with
rucksacs. Very helpful person.

Rab Carrington
Unit 16a Meersbrook Works
Valley Road, Heeley
Sheffield s8 9FT
Telephone (0742) 589144

Small firm who will sell down.
Will sell empty Shells for
Sleeping Bags for your Down to
fill at home. Very helpful.

DESMO Roof Racks
Joseph Billington
Providence Street
Cradley Heath
Worley, West Midlands

Spares for roof racks.

 # USEFUL CONTACT ADDRESSES

SHIRLEY INSTITUTE
Didsbury, Manchester M20 8RX
Large textile research with an international reputation.

BRITISH STANDARDS INSTITUTE
2 Park Street, London W1A 2BS. Telephone 01-629 9000
Responsible for all British Standards.

■ BOOK LIST

As far as I am aware there are no books currently in print that
deals with making clothing equipment for expeditions.
This list contains books about clothing and clothing technology.

The best book for our purpose is the book by Renbourn and Rees.

Brain R.   Primitive Environment
                                G. Philip London.

Cook J. G.   Handbook of Textile Fibres
                                W.S. Cowell, Ipswich.

Ewing E.   Dress and Undress
                                Batsford 1978

Hillary E. Doig D.   High in the Thin Cold Air
                                Hodder and Stoughton

Kerslake D. Mck.   The Stress of Hot Environments
                                Cambridge University Press.

Newburg L. H.   Physiology of Heat Regulation
                                Saunders 1949

Renbourn E. T.   Materials and Clothing in Health
and Rees W. H.   and Disease
                                Lewis and Co. London 1972

Russell M.   The Blessings of a Good Thick Skirt
                                Collins 1968

Smart J. and Griffiths   Covering Up
                                Science Museum London

Unsworth W.   Everest
                                Penguin Books

Saint-Laurient   A History of Ladies Underwear
                                Michael Joseph 1966

REFERENCES

Performance Testing of Outdoor Fabrics
J.H. Everest
Textile Institute and Industry
Vol.16, No.10, Oct 1978.

Breathable Fabrics and Comfort in Clothing
J.H. Keighley
Journal of Coated Fabrics.
Vol.15, Oct 1985.

Coated Fabrics – Light Weight Breathable
G.R. Lomas
Journal of Coated Fabrics.
Vol.15, Oct 1985.

IDENTIFYING FIBRES

The system described here is a simple method to identify fibres. If a fabric has been coated, the coating will affect the result. Look at the edge of a fabric (selvedge) for fibres that have not been coated.

First look under a microscope. Just a few fibres on a slide.

Look for	Fibre Type
Natural Fibres	
Scales on surface. Sections irregular. Sometimes a central canal.	Animal fibres, e.g. wool, mohair, rabbit, goat-hair, etc.
Fibres flat convoluted ribbons.	Cotton fibre.
Smooth and lustrous sections are triangular. Two filaments in raw.	Silk.
Coarse fibres.	Plant fibres (flax, hemp, jute).

Man-made Fibres

Lines along the fibres (striations). Serrated or lobed sections.	Viscose (Fibro, Sarille, Evlan), Acetate (Dicel, Triacetate) (Tricel).
Smooth, faint pitting on surface. Round or bean-shaped sections.	Modal (Vincel).
Smooth with round sections.	Nylon, polyester, polypropylene, polythene.
Wrinkled surface round section.	Acrylic (Courtelle).
Section off-round, bean-shaped or dog-bone shaped.	Modacrylic (Teklan, Verel), Acrylic (Acrilan, Orlon, Dralon).
Sections irregular folded lobes.	Modacrylic (Dynel).

To see cross-sections of fibres under a microscope, drill a hole in a thin sheet of metal, diameter of the hole should be about 1 mm.

Pull a bundle of fibres through the hole, then cut the surplus from each side of the metal plate with a sharp razor blade.

 # IDENTIFYING FIBRES

Burning Tests
(Coating and finishes will affect the results)

Fibres do not melt

Burns leave hard black residue. Smell of burnt hair.	Wool, silk, and hair fibres.
Burns readily, leaves grey ash. Smell of burnt paper.	Cotton, flax, hemp, jute, sisal, Viscose, Modal (Vincel).
Burns slowly, flame goes out when removed from flame. Black residue. Pungent smell.	Flame retardant viscose or Cellulose fibres with flame-retardant finish.
Burns readily leaving dark skeletal residue fishy smell.	Cellulose with resin finish, e.g. cotton or viscose.

Fibres melt

Burns rapidly, no soot, self-extinguishing.	Acetate (Dicel), Triacetate (Tricel).
Burns with difficulty, hard bead, smell of celery. Self-extinguishing.	Nylon 6 (Enkalon, Celon, Perlon). Nylon 6.6.
Burns with sooty flame, forms hard bead, sweet smell, self-extinguishing.	Polyester (Terylene, Dacron, Trevira).
Burns with spluttering, sooty flame, leaves irregular, crisp black mass, self-extinguishing.	Acrylic (Orlon, Acrilan, Courtelle, Dralon).

If you wish to study the identification of fibres further then you can purchase from "The Shirley Institute", Wilmslow Road, Manchester M20 8SA, a Fibre Sections Kit, and a kit of Stains to identify fibres.

A book "Identification of Textile Materials" is published by The Textile Institute, 10 Blackfriars Street, Manchester M3 5DR.

When you realise that there are over 1000 chemically different fibres in the world, which can be mixed together, which can be dyed with many different dyes, which can be woven or knitted to make fabrics which are finished in a variety of ways, and may then be coated with a variety of chemicals, you can appreciate that identifying unknown textile material is not a simple task.